T0311778

The Mature Student's Guide to Completing a Doctorate

Carefully structured to make it accessible and easy to follow, this thought-provoking book encourages the reader to facilitate a dialogue across disciplines so that mature and unconventional students are acknowledged and can discover a successful path towards admission and PhD completion. Based on real experiences of navigating the doctoral system, the guide includes insights from doctorates, candidates, supervisors, and examiners, who share their stories, insights, and advice. It covers key topics such as:

- Developing a research topic, conducting research, and research integrity
- Effectiveness, productivity, and progress
- Exploring key concepts and techniques through reading, writing, and networking
- Self-care and motivation
- Finding your academic voice

This guide is a must-read for advanced academic researchers, advanced postgraduate students, and experienced professionals with vocational backgrounds who are seeking recognition for their knowledge and alternative pathways to contribute to the sector.

Sinéad Hewson completed her PhD as a part-time student in 2021 and has lectured at Webster University, USA (Leiden Campus), Rotterdam School of Applied Sciences, the Netherlands, and TU Dublin, Ireland. She is the founder of an impact start-up in the Netherlands and works internationally on transformation, business scale-ups, and high performance.

Routledge Study Skills

The Mature Student's Guide to Completing a Doctorate
Sinéad Hewson

The Student Wellbeing Toolkit
Preparing for Life at College, University and Beyond
Camila Devis-Rozental

Writing a Postgraduate Thesis or Dissertation
Tools for Success
Michael Hammond

Studying Online
Succeeding through Distance Learning at University
Graham Jones

For more information about this series, please visit: https://www.routledge.com/Routledge-Study-Skills/book-series/ROUTLEDGESS

The Mature Student's Guide to Completing a Doctorate

Sinéad Hewson

Routledge
Taylor & Francis Group

LONDON AND NEW YORK

Designed cover image: © Henrik Sorensen/Getty Images

First published 2024
by Routledge
4 Park Square, Milton Park, Abingdon, Oxon OX14 4RN

and by Routledge
605 Third Avenue, New York, NY 10158

Routledge is an imprint of the Taylor & Francis Group, an informa business

© 2024 Sinéad Hewson

The right of Sinéad Hewson to be identified as author of this work has been asserted in accordance with sections 77 and 78 of the Copyright, Designs and Patents Act 1988.

British Library Cataloguing-in-Publication Data
A catalogue record for this book is available from the British Library

Library of Congress Cataloging-in-Publication Data
Names: Hewson, Sinéad, 1966- author.
Title: The mature student's guide to completing a doctorate / Sinéad Hewson.
Description: First edition. | New York : Routledge, 2024. |
Series: Routledge study skills | Includes bibliographical references and index. |
Identifiers: LCCN 2023051511 (print) | LCCN 2023051512 (ebook) | ISBN 9781032538013 (hbk) | ISBN 9781032538006 (pbk) | ISBN 9781003413691 (ebk)
Subjects: LCSH: Adult college students--Services for--Handbooks, manuals, etc. | Doctoral students--Handbooks, manuals, etc. | Universities and colleges--Graduate work--Handbooks, manuals, etc. | Interdisciplinary approach in education.
Classification: LCC LC5215 .H455 2024 (print) | LCC LC5215 (ebook) | DDC 378.1/9824--dc23/eng/20240123
LC record available at https://lccn.loc.gov/2023051511
LC ebook record available at https://lccn.loc.gov/2023051512

ISBN: 978-1-032-53801-3 (hbk)
ISBN: 978-1-032-53800-6 (pbk)
ISBN: 978-1-003-41369-1 (ebk)

DOI: 10.4324/9781003413691

Typeset in Warnock Pro
by SPi Technologies India Pvt Ltd (Straive)

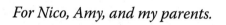

For Nico, Amy, and my parents.

Contents

Figures

Tables

Preface

The Mature Student's Guide to Completing a Doctorate helps candidates returning to academia and those working outside of education to proactively manage and complete their doctoral programmes, deliver superb work, and thrive. It is designed for individuals balancing multiple responsibilities and working part-time while studying.

These students face unique challenges such as limited time, access to valuable networks and resources, as well as caring responsibilities, change of circumstances and health. Their specific needs are partially addressed by their respective institutions. The quality of the experience often depends on the quality of the relationship with the supervisor and the level of engagement with the doctoral or graduate research department. The guide acts as a signpost for candidates to work in parallel with mentoring and peer support provided by universities. It is designed to mitigate the risk of stopping by bringing out the best in the candidate.

The book emerged from personal experience completing a part-time PhD. I know what self-doubt, tight deadlines, financial pressure, and social isolation feel like. I spent months navigating an environment I did not know and, even with support, wasted time trying to understand what was expected of me. Don't get me wrong, attempting to make sense of the unknown and the discomfort that ensues are valuable aspects of the doctoral experience. Nevertheless, there were occasions when my time could have been used more effectively elsewhere.

The content came together with the support and trust of peers and strangers who shared experiences, insights, and advice. I want to thank everyone who generously gave their time for one-to-one interviews. They included doctorates, candidates, supervisors, examiners, and individuals thinking about starting, some who deferred and some who did not complete their studies.

I hope the book is genuinely useful and helps you commit to the doctoral journey. At the end of the process, I hope that you deliver an exceptional body of work, share your knowledge, and have a positive impact on your community.

The doctoral experience will transform you. Embrace it and use the time well.

With best wishes,

Sinéad Hewson,

Voorschoten, The Netherlands.

5 October 2023.

PS: Update me on your progress. My contact details are at the end of the book.

Note: The words doctorate, doctoral, and PhD are interchanged throughout the book.

Acknowledgements

Thank you to family, friends, colleagues, and strangers who shared their experience, know-how, and advice.

Permissions

Resources

The draft manuscript was written on Scrivener, and the final edits were completed using Microsoft Word (text font, tables, spelling, sense check, accessibility, and plagiarism check).

Grammarly spell check, sense check, and plagiarism functions were used as editing resources at the end of the writing process.

Canva Magic Write was tested and utilised to sense check the section on logical fallacies towards the end of the writing process.

Disclaimer

The information in this book is provided as a guide for potential and current doctoral candidates. It addresses individual needs and does not replace the support offered by the institution awarding the doctorate. Seek the advice of your supervisor, mentor, and trusted points of contact to confirm that you follow programme guidelines appropriately and healthily.

The publisher and author make no guarantees concerning doctoral completion for individuals following the strategies and advice in the book. You, as the reader, acknowledge that individual outcomes can differ.

The references section of the chapters contains a number of third-party products, services, and resources for illustrative purposes. They are the property of their respective owners. Inclusion of a product, service, or resource does not represent an endorsement or recommendation to use by the author or publisher.

Introduction

INSIGHTS

"A PhD study does not really have an 'expiration date' as to when you can pursue it, I would say the contrary, it shows qualities such as commitment, determination, motivation and of course, a mind of enquiry, which can enable you to strengthen your profile."

Professor, supervisor, Head of Department,
Computer Science

▶ INTRODUCTION

The purpose of *The Mature Student's Guide to Completing a Doctorate* is to help candidates who are returning to academia and those working outside of education to proactively manage and complete their programmes, deliver superb work, and thrive. It is specifically designed for individuals balancing multiple responsibilities while working on their doctorate part-time.

The study guide results from a collaborative effort by the author and a diverse group of supporters, including doctorates, candidates, supervisors, examiners, and individuals thinking about starting, some who deferred, and some who did not complete their

DOI: 10.4324/9781003413691-1

studies. At the beginning of the development process, I explored whether candidates with limited academic experience or from under-represented groups are appropriately supported within current doctoral systems. The literature on the experience of candidates who don't quite fit the standard profile is examined from an institutional/academic perspective rather than the lens of someone going through the process.

There is a difference between intellectualisation of a topic, the phenomenon itself, and seeking ways to address it. For example, although the discomfort of adjusting to a new learning environment and imposter syndrome is acknowledged in the literature, the experiences of first-generation, part-time candidates, and those undertaking programmes remotely have been overlooked and they are "invisible" in research, policy, and the delivery of services specific to their needs. Some commentators argue that universities are "struggling to recognise the phenomenon" and adopt the beneficial aspects of distance programmes. They tend to leave it up to the candidates to make it work. The book hopes to address some of those unmet needs (Neumann & Rodwell, 2009; The Times Higher Education, 2023).

There was also an analysis of doctoral information sources such as university handbooks, articles, books, platforms and podcasts, and observation of peer group activity in open online forums. In addition, there was an examination of support resources and services for doctoral candidates. This was followed up with a series of one-to-one interviews and a number of formal and informal conversations on the doctoral experience. The feedback influenced the content, structure, and usefulness of the book, whose sole purpose is to help candidates focus and deliver an exceptional body of work.

Four doctoral completion triggers were identified: *motivation*, *organisation*, *progress*, and *wellbeing*. The book is divided into four parts with a total of 13 chapters containing insights from those who oversee, have completed, or are going through the doctoral process. A selection of exercises, role plays, actions, and resources that potentially aid progression are also included.

Readers are provoked to consider why they are undertaking a doctorate and the meaning, impact, and integrity of the proposed study. The "burden of representation" for those who emerge as first-generation doctorates within a family, group, community, profession, or sector is also discussed. This aspect of self and identity, according to participants, needs to be formally acknowledged within the academic experience and requires careful attention to mitigate the risk of dropping out.

The chapters are structured as follows:

Chapter 1: Introduction

Part I: Motivation
Chapter 2: Focus on the why

Part II: Organisation
Chapter 3: Approaches, resources, and requirements
Chapter 4: Planning and project management
Chapter 5: Research and critical thinking
Chapter 6: Thesis structure, literature review, and checklists

Part III: Progress
Chapter 7: Progress, mindsets, and momentum
Chapter 8: Writing and editing
Chapter 9: Staying on track and deadlines
Chapter 10: Feedback and setbacks
Chapter 11: The viva

Part IV: Wellbeing
Chapter 12: Focus on self
Chapter 13: Conclusion

Chapter 1: Introduction

The introduction chapter outlines the purpose of the study skills guide. It explains the motivation behind publishing the book, which is to help those returning to academia or part-time doctorates to complete their programmes. The benefits of advanced academic study and research on a personal, scholarly, and societal level are also highlighted. The chapter closes with a summary of key concepts and recommended exercises. It introduces the theme of *Part I: Motivation*, which delves into the mindset and motivation of candidates who commit to a PhD.

▶ PART I: MOTIVATION

Chapter 2: Focus on the why

Motivation, the first trigger of doctoral completion, is presented in Part I (Chapter 2). It discusses how candidates can identify why they want to commit, demonstrate advanced expertise, and invest a significant amount of time to conduct in-depth research into a topic. When the motivation trigger is strong, it acts as a filter guiding candidates so that they make good choices. It can be used to reignite commitment to the process on days when they feel like giving up. The chapter closes with a summary of key concepts and recommended exercises. It introduces the theme of *Part II: Organisation,* focusing on organisation and the responsibility of owning and managing your doctoral journey.

▶ PART II: ORGANISATION

Chapter 3: Approaches, resources, and requirements

The second doctoral completion trigger, *organisation*, is discussed in this and the following chapters. A PhD is a significant project and requires sufficient time, energy, and attention to follow through to the very end. Approaches, resources, and requirements are discussed. In addition, owning the process and taking responsibility for the work necessary to complete a programme. It concludes with a summary of concepts, exercises, and practical advice from doctoral candidates before leading into the chapter on planning and project management.

Chapter 4: Planning and project management

PhDs are complex, non-linear, long-term projects, and it is easy to get lost in the paperwork, learn new skills, and work out what to do next. This section builds helps candidates develop a practical work plan, get organised, complete tasks, and recognise where they are in the doctoral process. A summary of concepts, exercises, and practical advice is given at the end of the chapter.

Chapter 5: Research and critical thinking

This chapter aims to help candidates work out what exactly their research topic is and consider in what way a topic can be examined so that the process of gathering information, analysing data, and articulating results can be synthesised into a superb body of work. Essential research skills such as curiosity, critical thinking, open-mindedness, and the ability to understand different points of view are explored. It also provides guidance on defining a research topic and what research means in practice. The chapter concludes with a summary of concepts, exercises, and practical advice that lay the groundwork for the section on the thesis structure and literature review.

Chapter 6: Thesis structure, literature review, and checklists

The format of a typical doctoral thesis is provided in this section to help candidates with the development and structure of their own dissertation or commentary document. The function of a literature review and the role it plays in shaping the development of the doctoral topic and the final body of work is also discussed. A number of concepts, exercises, and practical tips are provided throughout the chapter leading into *Part III: Progress*, which focuses on completion.

▶ PART III: PROGRESS

Chapter 7: Progress, mindsets, and momentum

This section introduces the *progress* doctoral completion trigger. Momentum, tracking progress, patience, accuracy, and perfectionism are briefly discussed. The chapter closes with useful insights, role plays, exercises, and self-reflection tasks.

This links into *Chapter 8: Writing and editing*, which discusses how to get the work in a coherent and logical format so that it contributes to scholarly knowledge.

Chapter 8: Writing and editing

Finding an academic voice and the power of writing to demonstrate expertise rather than perfection is discussed. Techniques to aid completion are given so that candidates can present written material that is authentic, well-constructed, purposeful, understandable, and properly referenced. The chapter closes with useful insights, exercises, and self-reflection tasks before moving to *Chapter 9: Staying on track and deadlines*.

Chapter 9: Staying on track and deadlines

Practical issues such as staying on track, deadlines, timeliness, and adaptability are covered in this section. In addition, helpful strategies, tools, and insights are shared, they are focused on completion and aim to help candidates recognise when to stop, start, or change direction. This helps set the context for chapter 9, which addresses feedback and setbacks.

Chapter 10: Feedback and setbacks

This section examines how well-considered, constructive feedback aids completion and suggests a number of strategies to adopt when there are setbacks, unexpected delays, and challenges that might crop up during the doctoral process. The chapter closes with useful insights, role plays, exercises, and self-reflection tasks before moving on *to Chapter 11: The viva*. The feedback and setbacks chapter is closely aligned with *Part IV: Wellbeing*.

Chapter 11: The viva

This chapter is practically orientated and structured so that candidates can prepare for their viva voce (also known as a defence).

The viva voce is a formal process where doctoral candidates present and defend their work. It is an opportunity to engage with peers and demonstrate in-depth expertise, knowledge, and know-how as the doctoral programme finishes. Preparing for a viva voce requires clarity of thought and deciding the best way to showcase four to seven years of work into a 40-minute presentation, anticipate and respond to probing questions, and receive feedback to make the body of work stronger.

▶ PART IV: WELLBEING

Chapter 12: Focus on self

Managing breakthroughs and setbacks while balancing academic responsibilities with day-to-day life is candidly discussed in *Chapter 12: Focus on self*. The final doctoral completion trigger, *wellbeing*, suggests that when life gets in the way, it is okay to stop, reassess, and pivot to complete your PhD. This introduces the closing chapter, which reflects on the positive transformation experienced by doctorates after their conferring.

Chapter 13: Conclusion

The final chapter highlights a number of ways that excellence, the advancement of new ideas, and the ability to challenge preconceptions and enrich academic discourse are demonstrated. Finishing a lengthy project such as a PhD, examining intricate concepts through critical analysis, reviewing the literature, and collaborating effectively with others can have a greater impact on the candidate than the content of the thesis itself. The book closes with a call to action to seriously consider the benefits of starting a doctoral programme. It says to readers, if the timing is right, go for it.

▶ USING THE STUDY GUIDE

There are various ways to use the book. You can follow the order of the chapters, search for a specific term, or access information based on where you are in the doctoral process. It can be read in the same order as the doctoral guidelines provided by your institution using the index as a quick reference.

I recommend that you read and complete the exercises in *Part I: Motivation* (Chapter 2) before, during, and after the doctorate to understand the *why* behind this major life commitment. *Part II: Organisation* (Chapters 3, 4, 5, and 6) also provides checklists that can help with organisation, monitoring progress, and the structure of your final submission. *Part III: Progress* (Chapters 7, 8, 9, 10, and 11) is especially useful for navigating, processing feedback and gaining insight into the academic mindset. Lastly, *Part IV: Wellbeing* (Chapter 12) should be accessed continuously as it encourages self-care for a healthy, safe, and sustainable doctoral experience.

▶ BENEFITS AND EXPECTATIONS

Types of doctorates

A doctorate or PhD demonstrates in-depth knowledge in a specific field and the highest academic award.

Doctor of Philosophy (PhD) is the most common academic doctorate. It is awarded for original research and scholarship and focuses on expanding theoretical knowledge in traditional academic subject areas. The process involves completing coursework, conducting research, passing a theoretical exam, publishing a peer-reviewed manuscript, presenting at academic conferences, and submitting a detailed thesis.

Other types of doctoral degrees, such as a *PhD by prior publication* or a creative *portfolio*, require experienced candidates to demonstrate prior learning and expertise through analysis and presentation of their portfolio of work. The relationship is between the student and the institution.

The *professional doctorate* is practical in nature, and awards work that directly contributes to knowledge or improves practice in a specific field. This is achieved through original research, critical analysis, practical training, and instruction. Typically, one or more candidates, together with an academic supervisor and a collaborating company, work on an independent research project to address a live industry challenge. Most of the work is carried out on the premises of the collaborating company.

An *honorary doctorate* is awarded at the discretion of a university in recognition of individual achievement or contribution to a sector or society.

This guide focuses on earned doctoral degrees.

Learning goals

The learning goals of earned doctoral degrees, known as programme learning goals (PLGs), require that candidates demonstrate in-depth knowledge in a specialised area and contribute to knowledge worthy of publication and peer review (i.e. knowledge and understanding). They must complete a significant project over a prolonged period and demonstrate their research skills by designing, conducting, and analysing research. They must also show they can think critically, analyse, act with integrity, and demonstrate independence as a researcher/academic (i.e. applying knowledge and understanding and making judgements). They must also demonstrate that they can communicate findings and research conclusions to peers and a general audience (i.e. communication and learning skills).

Learning goals are usually based on supervisor and faculty feedback and, at the institutional level, they align with international qualification standards defining PhD/doctorate awards. In Europe, a doctorate signifies the completion of the third cycle of education. It is awarded to students who demonstrate a systematic understanding of a field of study and mastery of the skills and research methods in that field. These skills and abilities are collectively referred to as the Dublin Descriptors. (See Table 1.1 Doctoral learning outcomes).

Doctoral degree outcomes

TABLE 1.1 Doctoral learning outcomes

Outcomes for a doctoral degree (example)

A candidate is required to demonstrate the following:

1. KNOWLEDGE AND UNDERSTANDING

1.2 Broad knowledge and understanding of their research field/ subject matter area.

1.3 In-depth, up-to-date specialist knowledge and state-of-the-art in a particular area.

2. PROFICIENCY AND ABILITY

2.1 Critically analyse, examine, and review facts, issues, and situations.

2.2 Operate with intellectual independence. Act ethically and with integrity.

2.3 Identify and formulate research questions critically, objectively, and creatively.

2.4 Design, plan and conduct research adopting appropriate methods with scientific rigour.

2.5 Complete tasks and reach milestones in a timely manner.

2.6 Review and evaluate the work and articulate the findings.

2.7 A significant contribution to knowledge development by completing a substantial project and (depending on the type of doctorate) writing a thesis and/or several academic articles or commentary of prior publication/portfolio.

2.8 Communicate by presenting and discussing the research, results, and the case for examination orally and in writing amongst peers and the general public nationally and internationally.

2.9 Present work logically and coherently following international codes of practice.

2.10 Contribute to society and support the learning of others.

3. JUDGEMENT AND APPROACH

3.1 Act with intellectual independence, (research) integrity.

3.2 The ability to make ethical decisions and judgements.

3.3 Personal accountability.

3.4 Insight into the potential and limitations of the research and science in general.

Content adapted from multiple sources, including:

European Code for Research Integrity 2017 and 2023; Karolinska Institutet 2023; National Framework for Doctoral Education, HEA 2017; Articulating learning outcomes in doctoral education. Washington, DC: Council of Graduate Schools 2017; The PhD Viva, P. Smith 2014; Borrell-Damian, L. (2009); European Higher Education Area & Bologna Process 2005; The Higher Education Ordinance, Annexe 2, Sweden, 1993.

IMPORTANT: This framework is for illustration purposes only. Universities may have additional requirements and highlight specific skill sets necessary to meet award criteria.

Commitment

Doctoral degrees can be completed full-time or part-time, and depending on programme requirements, participation can be in-person, virtually or in a hybrid format. Earned doctorates, in general, take 3–4 years to complete full-time and up to seven years part-time, resulting in a thesis of 40,000–80,000 words and/or a specific number of publications in academic journals, while accelerated programmes such as a doctorate by prior publication can last 2–3 years with an obligation to submit a critique and analysis of 10,000–20,000 words.

Completion rates

Although the completion rate for doctoral programmes varies, completion rates increase when the following elements are in place: financial support, a supportive academic and personal environment, affinity with the research topic, a strong academic adviser relationship, candidate readiness, and a clear understanding of expectations and goals.

The literature review, market and environmental scan, and one-to-one interviews for the book identified several triggers for completion, deferral, and dropout (Table 1.2). They are *motivation, organisation, progress,* and *wellbeing.*

Completion triggers

Doctoral-level research focuses on the exploration of new concepts and ideas. Scholars employ problem-solving strategies, interpret data, use philosophical and ethical reasoning to solve puzzles, and understand abstract concepts. As the programme of study progresses, the process may not be as straightforward as anticipated. Candidates, as well as experienced researchers, express discomfort, believing the process should be easier to navigate because they already have in-depth knowledge. The candidates interviewed for the book said that although the process of discovery, deep thinking, and learning new things in new ways can be uncomfortable, it is worth the effort.

TABLE 1.2 Triggers for completion, deferral, and dropout

Completion trigger	Dropout/deferral risk with limited/lack of
Motivation	Understanding the motivation to undertake a doctorate. Affinity with the research topic. Candidate readiness. Understanding of expectations and goals.
Organisation	Understanding of expectations. Organisation and systems. Access to resources and tools. SMART goals. Supportive academic, personal, and physical environment. Financial support.
Process	Understanding of the current status of the project. Reliable systems and processes. Tracking tasks, results, milestones, and progress. Time and budget management. Resources, tools, and access.
Wellbeing	Supportive academic and personal environment. Ownership of the doctoral process. Proactive management of health and wellbeing.

INSIGHT

"You will live with the doctoral work for several years. On the days you want to stop. Take a break and remind yourself why you are putting yourself through this."

Part-time doctoral candidate, History

"It has opened new doors for me."

Part-time doctoral candidate, Theology

▶ SUMMARY

This chapter explains the structure of the study guide and briefly outlines the level of commitment and standards demanded at doctoral level. Completion, underpinned by the state of *motivation, organisation, progress, and wellbeing* in a candidate is necessary.

Themes covered in the introduction chapter include:

Completion triggers
Doctoral types
Imposter syndrome
Doctoral learning outcomes
Using the guide

▶ USEFUL RESOURCES AND REFERENCES

References

ALLEA. (2023). *The European Code of Conduct for research integrity – Revised Edition 2023.* Berlin. doi:10.26356/ECOC; ISBN: 978-3-9823562-3-5.

Borrell-Damian, L. (2009). *Collaborative Doctoral Education. University-industry partnerships for enhancing knowledge exchange. DOC-CAREERS Project.* Brussels: EUA. ISBN: 9789078997139.

Denecke, D., Kent, J., & McCarthy, M.T. (2017). *Articulating learning outcomes in Doctoral Education.* Washington, DC: Council of Graduate Schools. ISBN: 10-digit 1-933042-51-6 13-digit 978-1-933042-51-0.

European Higher Education Area. (2005). https://www.ehea.info/media. ehea.info/file/WG_Frameworks_qualification/85/2/Framework_qualificationsforEHEA-May2005_587852.pdf

HEA. (2017). *National Framework for Doctoral Education.* https://hea.ie/assets/uploads/2017/04/national_framework_for_doctoral_education_0.pdf

Neumann, R., & Rodwell, J. (2009). The "invisible" part-time research students: A case study of satisfaction and completion. *Studies in Higher Education, 34* (1), 55–68. doi:10.1080/03075070802601960

Smith, P. (2014). *The PhD viva* (1st ed.). Bloomsbury Publishing. New York. ISBN: 9781137395764.

The Higher Education Ordinance. (1993). *Annexe 2*, Sweden. https://www.uhr.se/en/start/laws-and-regulations/Laws-and-regulations/The-Higher-Education-Ordinance/Annex-2/

The Times Higher Education. (2023). *Distance doctoral students 'invisible' to universities.* https://www.timeshighereducation.com/news/distance-doctoral-students-invisible-universities

Resources

ALLEA. (2023) https://allea.org/

Discover PhDs. (2023). https://www.discoverphds.com/advice/doctorates

Karolinska Institutet. (2023). https://staff.ki.se/outcomes-for-doctoral-education-according-to-the-higher-education-ordinance

Part I
Motivation

2

Focus on the why

INSIGHTS

"I did the bachelor's for my parents, the master's for my employer and the PhD for me."

PhD, Entrepreneurship

"The PhD is for me."

PhD, History

"I wanted to prove to myself that I could do it."

PhD, Communication

"When I was told we don't accept women because they leave to have children, I found a way around it to make it happen by finding the right supervisor."

PhD, Psychology

"There are people in my church community who are living with dementia, and I wanted to do something about."

PhD, Theology

"You need a doctorate to advance your career."

PhD, History

"It is a lonely journey. And if you are not self-motivated, you can easily give up."

PhD, Theology

DOI: 10.4324/9781003413691-3

▶ INTRODUCTION

The fundamental message of this chapter is that in order to complete a doctoral programme, you need a compelling reason to do the work and be fully aware of the level of commitment required to progress through each stage. The interviews with doctorates and supervisors highlighted that making a positive contribution and creating new knowledge is the primary driver. Completing is underpinned by resilience and persistence expressed as "I need to prove to myself that I can do this".

A number of role plays and exercises follow, they are designed to help identify and connect with your motivation to start a PhD, and to explore the strength of belief, affinity, and connection you have with the research topic and what it means for you to complete. The exercises in this chapter focus on *motivation* (the why) and *mindset* (the attitude to keep going). Throughout the remainder of the book, *action* (impactful steps towards completion) exercises are shared.

▶ PIVOTING

The word pivot has several meanings (the central point on which something depends, to turn or rotate and to completely change direction). The Pivoting Model (Figure 2.1) presented in the book contains a series of incremental exercises that are spread throughout the chapters. It aims to help readers understand and connect with their (i) personal *motivation* (the *why*), (ii) the *mindset* needed to follow up and commit to a doctoral programme, and (iii) the *actions* necessary to set an intention, progress, and reach your goal. This is a critical step for part-time, under-represented, and mature candidates because when there is a compelling reason to complete, change happens (see Tables 2.1, 2.2, 2.3, 2.5, and 2.6).

The model allows readers to explore their *motivation* and identify the primary reason for taking a particular course of action or

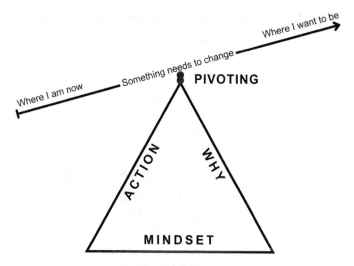

Figure 2.1 Pivoting Model © 2019–2023 Sinéad Hewson created with Canva.com

behaving in a particular way. The first exercise asks *where you are now* and *where you want to be*. This helps to create a sense of purpose that *something needs to change*. Then there is an exploration of what *makes you get up in the morning* and then you reflect on how these insights can help you complete your doctorate. This is an important completion driver.

Exercise: Pivoting I: Something needs to change

Review the text in Table 2.1 Pivoting I. Something needs to change. Sit somewhere where you won't be disturbed for about two hours. Get a notepad, pen, and something (healthy) to drink and complete the exercise.

For a guided audio recording of this exercise, go to the resources section of www.unconventionaldoctorates.com

TABLE 2.1 Exercise: Pivoting I. Something needs to change

STEP 1: Reality check	Be honest with yourself:
Duration: 45 mins	1. Where are you now? 2. What needs to change to get where you want to be? 3. Be mindful; notice what appears.
STEP 2: Reflect/Meditate	Identify:
Duration: 45–90 mins **Tip**: Write or record the first things that come to mind.	1. The reasons I get up in the morning. 2. What makes my heart sing? 3. What gives me joy? 4. What do I love? 5. What am I good at? 6. What can I be paid for 7. What gap can I fill? 8. Where can I make a difference? 9. Be mindful; notice what appears.
STEP 3: Write/Record	Summarise:
Duration: 15–30 mins	1. What are the three most useful insights from this task? 2. How will these insights help you with your doctorate?
WHERE AM I NOW?	

Pivoting I. Something needs to change © 2019–2023 Sinéad Hewson.

INSIGHTS

"My goal was to pursue a doctorate after I finished my Masters's degree, but the timing wasn't right at the time, so I started working and gaining experience having in the back of my mind that whenever I have a good opportunity I will get it."

PhD, Sustainability

Exercise: Pivoting II. Maintaining balance

This exercise uses the Wheel of Life® framework (Figure 2.2) developed by Paul J. Mayer in the 1960s to scan and identify areas of your life that might require special attention during the doctoral programme. The exercise has been adapted for use by doctoral candidates. Repeat every six to twelve months, and consider practical ways insights gained from this exercise can help you progress.

TABLE 2.2   Exercise: Pivoting II. Maintaining balance

STEP 1: Reality check **Duration**: 5 mins	Document the first answer that springs to mind. On a scale of 0–10 (where 0 is the lowest and 10 is the highest score), what mark would I give in this area of my life?
	Health and wellbeing _____ Money _____ Career _____ Friends and family _____ Recreation and fun _____ Personal and spiritual growth _____ Physical environment _____ Significant other(s) _____
STEP 2: Reflect/Meditate **Duration**: 15–30 mins	1. Which sections have the highest and lowest scores? 2. Mark the scores with an x in each spoke of the Wheel of Life® diagram (Figure 2.2 Wheel of Life®) (0 is at the centre of the diagram). 3. Join the dots and notice the shape. 4. What are the priorities you need to work on?
STEP 3: Record **Duration**: 15–30 mins	Summarise/write 1. What are the three most useful insights from this task? 2. How will these insights help you with your doctorate?

IN WHAT WAY CAN THESE INSIGHTS HELP ME COMPLETE MY DOCTORATE?

Wheel of Life® is a registered trademark of Success Motivation® International, Inc. Pivoting II. Maintaining Balance © 2019–2023 Sinéad Hewson.

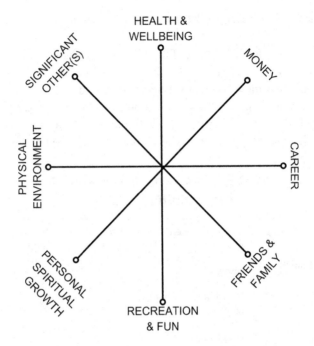

Figure 2.2 Wheel of Life® is a registered trademark of Success Motivation® International, Inc. © 2023 Sinéad Hewson created with Canva.com

For a guided audio recording of this exercise, go to the resources section of www.unconventionaldoctorates.com

▶ MINDSET

> "There are no great achievements without setbacks"
>
> Dweck 2017

The relationship between maturity and wisdom was first documented by Cicero in 44 BC (Cicero 44 BC/1951). He believed that older individuals possess practical wisdom and reasoning abilities that can resolve conflict and enrich civic society. In contrast, Cattel proposes that there are two forms of intelligence, fluid intelligence (Gf) refers to the ability to reason and think flexibly, independent of learning, experience, and education, while crystallised intelligence (Gc) encompasses the knowledge, facts, and skills acquired throughout life (Cattell, 1963). Crystallised intelligence was cited as a benefit of starting a PhD later in life by interview participants who said their younger selves were not mature enough to think critically and navigate the doctoral system. Social scientist Arthur C. Brooks work acknowledges this point of view suggesting that, as people age, they become more skilled at combining and utilising complex ideas and that they know what to do with complex information (Brooks 2022).

I call the deepening of wisdom, a willingness to learn, create and share knowledge sageism.

Growth and Fixed Mindsets

A Growth Mindset is the belief that people can develop their abilities, it is fostered through hard work, strategies, focus, and perseverance (Dweck 2006). Many institutional programmes encourage candidates to adopt a Growth Mindset as a means to enable curiosity, deep thinking, and critical analysis, which can contribute to scholarly discourse. In a Fixed Mindset, there is a belief that abilities, talents, or qualities are fixed traits with a focus on documenting rather than developing intelligence or talent.

Reflections by mature students returning to academia highlight an internal belief by some that they are perceived as dinosaurs, lacking ideas and unwilling to change. However, interview participants said that, in reality, this is not the case, "the perspective we bring is incredibly" and a strength. To do so, there is a requirement to adopt a Growth Mindset, be open to feedback, actively listen, and welcome scholarly advice and criticism.

> "Sometimes, mature PhD candidates possess a good deal of knowledge to execute their research from their work experience but they haven't had the chance to label and structure their knowledge to make it actionable for the PhD".
> Professor, supervisor, Head of Department,
> Computer Science

Dweck says that adopting a Growth Mindset (Figure 2.3) means there is an inherent belief that intelligence can be developed, leading to a desire to learn and embrace challenges in the face of setbacks. Effort is required on the path to mastery. This includes learning from criticism and finding inspiration in the success of

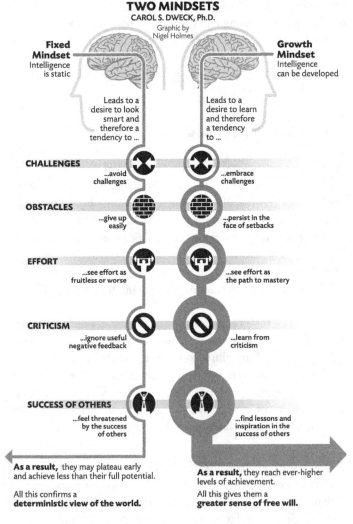

Figure 2.3 Two Mindsets by Professor Carol Dweck, graphic by Nigel Holmes

others, resulting in a higher level of achievement (Dweck, 2006, 2016, 2017; Forte, 2022).

A Fixed Mindset suggests that intelligence is static, which leads to a desire to look smart and a tendency to avoid challenges, give up easily, consider effort a fruitless endeavour, ignore useful or negative feedback, feel threatened by the success of others, and achieve less than their full potential. Interview participants recognised these traits within their own experience, expressing a pressure to be right, "not look like an idiot", or make stupid mistakes. This will be explored further when handling feedback and managing setbacks are discussed in Chapter 10.

As you advance through the programme, acknowledge that the doctoral process may not be as straightforward as anticipated. Even experienced researchers express discomfort, believing they should do better because they already have in-depth knowledge. The candidates interviewed for the book said although the process of discovery, deep thinking, and learning about new things in new ways can be uncomfortable and worth the effort, you may need to self-reflect on ways to "persuade our fixed mindset persona to get on board with goals that spring from our growth mindset" (Dweck 2017). The pull between fixed and growth-minded is expanded in *Part III: Progress.*

Exercise: How will my life change?

Once the joy of being accepted into a programme has passed, take a moment to step back and reflect on why you are doing this and what you are getting yourself into. A university information pack might say that over seven years, between eight to 20 hours a week of commitment is required. What does this mean to you and the people around you? In what ways could day-to-day life change during and after the process? And most important of all, how do you stay committed to a process that takes so long?

Find a place where you will not be disturbed for about two to three hours (longer if necessary). Reflect on what it is that you want to change and ask: What is my current situation? (Use the findings from the exercises Pivoting I. Something needs to change and Pivoting II. Maintaining balance.)

Write down the first things that spring to mind. Then go deeper by reviewing your words and then explore various aspects of your life using the Wheel of Life® terms as a prompt. They are health and wellbeing, money, career, friends and family, recreation and fun, personal spiritual growth, physical environment, and significant other(s). Take your time. Writing your thoughts on paper rather than typing transfers the information out of your head and into a format you can touch. Ignore typos and messiness, and keep writing. See what appears. Do you have a burning ambition to instil change in the area you work in? Are you an advocate for social change? Do you want to provide a brighter future for your family? Interview participants said, initially, I wanted to make a positive difference in an area I am passionate about, but ultimately, I did it for myself, I had to prove to myself that I could do this. Notice what comes up and consider how these insights will aid your completion.

An alternative approach to complete this exercise is to record it on a smartphone or as if you are on a Zoom call with a trusted friend or mentor. Then, talk to the camera as if you are talking to your future self (10 years into the future) and see what insights appear. Use screen share, record, and caption functions to capture your thoughts.

Ask, what is my current situation? What am I good at? What is my challenge? What needs to change? The "something needs to change" insight allows you to develop the first version of your doctoral goal which will be refined throughout the programme.

Then consider, what is my goal (i.e. what is it and what will it look like)? And reflect, as I go through the doctoral process, how will I know I have achieved my goal? (i.e. what will be different? What will it look, feel, sound, and taste like?) And finally, what are the payoffs or benefits of achieving this goal?

A key factor in doctoral completion according to those interviewed is having an unwavering and deep connection with why you want to complete the research and doctoral programme (see Table 2.3). When the connection is strong, you become more resilient when handling setbacks and better able to identify the next steps or defend your actions. The following questions help test the level of conviction as you reflect on what will happen when you achieve your goal. What will be different, what will it look, feel, taste, and smell like? Then you are asked what will not happen or stop when you achieve your goal. Take a deep breath and then ask what will happen if you do not achieve your goal. And then consider what will stop/not happen if you do not achieve your goal. Reflect, refine your goal, and let the information sink in.

For a guided audio recording of this exercise go to the resources section of www.unconventionaldoctorates.com

Exercise: Pivoting III. Why should I change?

INSIGHTS

"I was hooked and wanted to know more."
PhD candidate quote (Borrell-Damian 2009)

"I was clear on my goal."
Part-time PhD by prior publication

TABLE 2.3 Exercise: Pivoting III. Why should I change?

STEP 1: Why? **Duration:** 30 mins	1. What is my current situation? 2. What am I good at? 3. What is my challenge? 4. What needs to change? 5. What is my goal? 6. How will I know I have achieved my goal? 7. What are the payoffs? 8. What will happen when I achieve my goal? 9. What will not happen/or stop when I achieve my goal? 10. What will happen if I do not achieve my goal? 11. What will not happen/or stop if I do not achieve my goal? 12. Reflect on what resonates and what makes you uncomfortable. Then refine the wording of your goal. 13. Close your eyes, take a deep breath, and allow the information to sink in.
STEP 2: Write/Record **Duration:** 15–30 mins	Summarise: 1. What are the three most useful insights from this task? 2. How will these insights help you with your doctorate?
STEP 3: Action **duration** as needed	**Insights:** 1. 2. 3. **How they help with the doctorate:** 1. 2. 3. **Actions:** 1. 2. 3. **Resources and support by when:** 1. 2. 3.

IN WHAT WAY CAN THESE INSIGHTS HELP ME COMPLETE MY DOCTORATE?

Mastery

There are different stages of mastery that individuals can reach when learning or doing something. Understanding this is a useful point of reference for candidates as they progress through their doctoral programme (see Table 2.4).

The *novice* stage is when someone is a beginner, they do not know how to do something and may not realise it. The *advanced beginner* stage is when someone performs to a basic standard and are not yet proficient. They are aware of their skills/knowledge gap and understand the value of learning, improving, and making mistakes. *Competence and proficiency*, occurs when someone has learned how to do something yet still needs to focus and put effort into doing it

TABLE 2.4 Stages of mastery/levels of competence

Mastery	Description
Novice	Unaware, lacks proficiency, unconscious incompetence: Does not know how to do something and may not realise it yet.
Advanced Beginner	Aware, not yet proficient, can perform to basic standards, conscious incompetence: Is aware of the skills/knowledge gap and recognises the value of learning and improvement.
Competent and gaining proficiency	Learning, takes effort to be competent, gaining experience, conscious competence. They know how to do something and need to put effort into doing it correctly. When focus is lost or the steps are unclear, they can revert to being unconsciously incompetent.
Mastery	Expertise, automatic, know-how, unconscious competence: They master a skill so well that they can do it without thinking and complete another task at the same time, depending on how they learned it.

Adapted from multiple sources including:

Trotter, R. (1986). The mystery of mastery. Psychology Today, 20 (7), 32–38.; Flower J. In the mush. Physician Executive 1999 Jan-Feb; 25 (1): 64–66. PMID: 10387273.; Ambrose, S. A., Bridges, M. W., DiPietro, M., Lovett, M. C., & Norman, M. K. (2010). How learning works. John Wiley & Sons.

correctly. When focus is lost or steps are unclear, or confusing, they revert to being unconsciously incompetent. The final stage of *mastery* is when someone has mastered a skill so well that they can do it without thinking about it. They possess expertise and know-how and are capable of teaching others. This is the level expected of a PhD.

Meditation/reflection

As the chapter closes, take a moment to reflect and take a pragmatic look at your potential future. Get out in the fresh air, walk in the park, by the beach, or go to your favourite place to reflect for a couple of hours. Reflect on your ideal day (see Table 2.5). Ask if the doctoral path is the right one for you. If you come to the conclusion that a PhD is right for you, explore the actions you need to take to complete the task (see Table 2.6).

For guided audio recordings of these exercises, go to the resources section of www.unconventionaldoctorates.com

Exercise: Pivoting IV. My ideal day

"When I completed the my ideal day exercise. I realised I had to balance caring my business, committing to the programme and completing the work. I organised chunks of time away from home with help from family and friends. Spending 2–3 days a month on campus and staying overnight allowed me to focus and successfully complete."

Part-time PhD, self-employed, and caregiver

"[As a family] We needed to pivot and adjust emotionally and be organised."

Part-time PhD, self-employed, and parent

"I have a family so I needed to work throughout my PhD. For the duration of my studies, there were no Christmas and family holidays for my kids who were young and could not understand my motivations."

Part-time PhD, full-time role, and parent

TABLE 2.5 Exercise: Pivoting IV.
My ideal day

A PhD is a commitment.

Take 30 minutes and write, draw, or create a collage outlining your ideal day and study week. Break it down hour by hour and consider your multiple responsibilities while completing the work.
It might start something like "I wake up at ... then I ... and then I ..."

Pivoting IV. My ideal day © 2008–2023 Sinéad Hewson.

Exercise: Pivoting V. Which path is right for me?

TABLE 2.6 Exercise: Pivoting V.
Which path is right for me?

1. Is a PhD for me?
2. On a scale of one to ten, how curious and excited am I?
3. What type of doctorate and study option would work best for me?
4. What institutions are highly rated within my specialist area?
5. What are the international rankings for the university?
6. What is the reputation of the faculty? Is there someone I specifically want to work with?
7. Is it accessible?
8. Is it affordable?
9. What other factors (costs, equipment, caring or work responsibilities etc.) need to be taken into account?
10. What is the value/benefits of attending this institution?
11. How easy is it to attend in person?
12. What options are available to participate?
13. Is it a practical option?
14. Will I like it there?
15. How will I make it work?
16. What are the benefits of joining the 2% club? (Less than 2% of the world's population has a PhD)
17. Anything else?

Take a deep breath and notice

1. Where are you now?
2. What needs to change to get where you want to be?
3. Be mindful; notice what appears.

Pivoting V. Which path right for me? © 2023 Sinéad Hewson.

> "Some candidates are drawn to study because it looks good. They don't necessarily understand what is expected of them. It is important to know if this path is the right one before you start."
>
> Part-time PhD, Diplomacy

Application checklist

If you decide, the answer is yes. Take time to research the right institution and supervisor to partner with for the next four to seven years, and give yourself ample time to complete the application (see Table 2.7).

TABLE 2.7 Application checklist

1. What is expected of me?
2. What do I need to do to complete the application?
3. Do I know someone who has successfully applied for a programme? Can I talk to them?
4. Who can help me?
5. What documentation, scans, and official documents do I need to include and in what format?
6. Is there an application cost?
7. What is the deadline?
8. Have I checked for errors/gaps? How do I address these?
9. Do I need to include a brief outline of what my research idea might be?
10. Anything else?

Application Checklist © 2023 Sinéad Hewson.

INSIGHTS

> "Open yourself up for growth."
>
> Dweck 2017

> "On the days you want to stop, focus on the why."
>
> Part-time PhD, History

> "In my case, I applied for a master's by research. My supervisor recommended that I move to the PhD track because of my industry knowledge and the thesis topic. I was invited to join the programme."
>
> PhD, Communication

▶ SUMMARY

The primary message from this chapter is that a compelling why underpins the successful completion of a doctoral programme. Part-time and first-generation candidates highlight that there is a sense of burden to show up and do the right thing and that it is up to them to make the most of the opportunities a PhD creates by being pro-active and owning the process. A compelling why keeps you going on the days you want to stop.

The themes covered this this chapter are:

Application Checklist
Fixed Mindset
From novice to mastery
Growth Mindset
Which path is right for me?
Motivation
My ideal day
Pivoting Model
What needs to change to get to where you want to be?

▶ USEFUL RESOURCES AND REFERENCES

References

Ambrose, S. A., Bridges, M. W., DiPietro, M., Lovett, M. C., & Norman, M. K. (2010). *How learning works*. New Jersey: John Wiley & Sons: ISBN: 978-0-470-48410-4.

Borrell-Damian, L. (2009). *Collaborative Doctoral Education. University-industry partnerships for enhancing knowledge exchange. DOC-CAREERS Project*. Brussels: EUA: ISBN: 9789078997139.

Brooks, A. C. (2022). *From strength to strength: Finding meaning, success, and deep purpose in the second half of life*. New York, NY: Portfolio/Penguin: ISBN: 059319148X; 978-0593191484.

Cattell, R. B. (1963). Theory of fluid and crystallized intelligence: A critical experiment. *Journal of Educational Psychology*, 54 (1), 1–22. doi:10.1037/h0046743.

Cicero M. T. (44 BC/1951). On old age. In Hadas M. (Ed.), *The basic works of Cicero* (pp. 125–158). New York, NY: The Modern Library. ISBN: 0394309553, 9780394309552.

Dweck, C. S. (2006). *Mindset: The new psychology of success.* New York: Random House: ISBN: 1400062756, 9781400062751, 9780345472328, 0345472322.

Dweck, C. S. (2016). What having a growth mindset actually means. *Harvard Business Review Online.*

Dweck, C. S. (2017). *Mindset - Updated edition: Changing the way you think to fulfil your potential* (p. 260). London: Little, Brown Book Group: Kindle Edition: ISBN: 978-1-47213-996-2.

Flower, J. (1999). In the mush. *Physician Executive*, 25 (1), 64–66. PMID: 10387273.

Forte, T. (2022). *Building a second brain: A proven method to organize your digital life and unlock your creative potential.* New York: Atria Books. Kindle Edition: ISBN: 9781982167387, 9781982167394, 9781982167400.

Trotter, R. (1986). The mystery of mastery. *Psychology Today*, 20 (7), 32–38.

Vitae (2004). Bologna Process: Dublin descriptors for the doctoral degree 2004 — Vitae Website. https://www.vitae.ac.uk/policy/dublin-descriptors-for-doctorate-mar-2004-vitae.pdf

Part II
Organisation

3 Approaches, resources, and requirements

INSIGHT

"Develop a concrete growth-orientated plan ... and stick to it."

Dweck 2017

▶ INTRODUCTION

This chapter focuses on the second doctoral completion trigger *organisation*. It argues that a PhD is a significant project and requires sufficient time, energy, and attention to follow through to the very end. A flexible framework is proposed to help candidates develop a practical work plan, get organised, complete tasks, and take responsibility for their work.

The chapter acknowledges that some candidates are unfamiliar with specific terms or academic processes. In situations where practical know-how is high and academic experience is low, it can be a challenge to fall in line and comply with academic regulations, standards, and practises. Therefore, the role of supervisors

DOI: 10.4324/9781003413691-5

to guide, mentor, and unlock potential is critical to avoid unnecessary tension and confusion.

The chapter highlights that mastery requires a significant investment of time, energy, and effort throughout the doctoral journey. Furthermore, there is a mindset shift towards curiosity and accuracy. One which embraces the unknown and learns from setbacks to enrich their findings. For instance, accurate word usage and language patterns combined with a clear articulation of academic outcomes build trust and credibility. The chapter closes with a summary of key concepts and recommended exercises and introduces the theme of *Part III: Progress.*

▶ WELL BEGUN IS HALF DONE

At first glance, obtaining a PhD may seem overwhelming. However, the key to success is to recognise that it is a long journey (Table 3.1 Generic doctoral/PhD timeline). It follows an incremental, disruptive process and aims to contribute to new knowledge. Completion requires effective organisation, a systemic approach, effective time management, and understanding why you are pursuing this.

▶ ADOPTING A DESIGN THINKING APPROACH TO YOUR DOCTORATE

Design Thinking is a people-centred iterative process used to understand a context, challenge assumptions, redefine problems and propose, and prototype and test innovative solutions. In doctoral studies, the approach can help candidates tackle problems that are ill-defined or unknown. It removes assumptions, throws the net wide, and identifies patterns, trends, and gaps in an area of expertise. In the early stage of a PhD, it can be used to filter ideas into potential areas of study that are of genuine interest to a candidate, as long as there is potential to genuinely contribute to new knowledge. The Design Council's Double Diamond framework

TABLE 3.1 Generic doctoral/PhD timeline

Timing	Item
START:	Acceptance invitation.
0–3 months full-time **0–1 year part-time**	**Registration.** Formal intake. Welcome, induction & and orientation, standards, guidelines and codes, where to go for support. Supervisor meeting.
	Proposal, work plan, or research agreement approved. Confirm institutional relationships and funding conditions. Confirm and sign supervision and work agreements, expectations, and doctoral education plan. Complete PhD agreement form. ORCID registration. Pre-registration of the proposed research (if applicable).
	The work plan is implemented.
MIDDLE: **4–42 months full-time** **2–4 years part-time**	**The work plan is updated and implemented.** Annual progress presentation. Transfer exam/mid-term progress presentation. Final progress presentation.
END: **42–48 months full-time** **4–7 years part-time**	**The work plan is updated and implemented.** Complete doctoral training programme. Exam committee. Plagiarism check. Submit manuscript. Viva voce/Preliminary defence. Edits. Approval of final manuscript. Complete.

helps visualise the doctoral journey where there are areas of divergence (expansion of ideas, information, and data) and convergence of information into themes, prototypes, and outputs.

Scalable part-time Doctoral Framework

A typical part-time doctorate takes 4–7 years to complete, and the diagram presents a scalable framework highlighting the key stages in the process that candidates should be aware of.

Most doctoral programmes follow a similar format. Candidates research a specific topic, analyse data, develop and connect ideas, articulate findings, and demonstrate their expertise. Throughout the process, there is a requirement to reflect and demonstrate the effect of the doctoral experience on the individual. This forms the basis of the annual review and thesis defence.

The Scalable part-time Doctoral Framework (Figure 3.1) indicates what is required and when for part-time candidates. Year one and two is the time when the doctoral topic is identified, a review of the literature takes place, and the research methodology/approach to the work is finalised. Ways of working are established, and training and annual reviews take place. In years two and three, momentum increases, the research takes place, and initial ideas and potential findings start to emerge. A formal evaluation (transfer exam) occurs around year three or four to check that the work undertaken meets doctoral requirements. Then, the remainder of the programme focuses on iterating ideas, and writing up findings, recommendations, and conclusions for delivery at conferences, in articles, and drafting the final thesis or commentary document. The key to completing is to recognise that it is not always a linear process, and to anticipate, plan, and aim to complete to the best of your ability. There are times when you will love the experience and times when you wonder what all the effort is for. Understanding where you are in the process helps maintain focus.

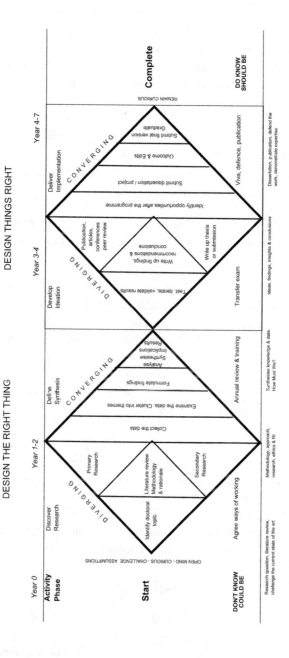

Figure 3.1 Scalable part-time Doctoral Framework based on a typical candidate's journey towards completion. © 2023 Sinéad Hewson created with Canva.com. The Double Diamond by the Design Council is licensed under a CC BY 4.0 license. Content is adapted to explain a typical doctoral journey.

Exercise: My Doctoral Framework

Review the doctoral framework in Figure 3.1. If you were creating your own version for your doctoral journey, what needs to change? How can it be customised? Realistically, how much time do you think it will take for you to complete your doctorate? Discuss this with your supervisor.

For a blank version of this template, go to the resources page of www.unconventionaldoctorates.com

---

INSIDER TIP

Treat your PhD as a project with a beginning, a middle, and an end. Good organisation helps maintain momentum and focus.

The one-to-one interviews highlighted the reasons why people invest in and return to academia to complete a PhD. It can be for self-development or because someone has been passed over in a promotion or their views are not taken seriously. It is an achievement to be accepted into a programme, and the critical next step is to focus on pivoting your lifestyle, work, and priorities so that you can complete on time and healthily.

It is beneficial to have a clear vision of who you want to become at the end of the process. Do you want to be recognised as an innovator and critical thinker and become the expert everyone wants to collaborate with? There are times when you will ask yourself: *Why am I putting myself, my family, and my friends through this?* Re-frame the question, and focus your attention on your intention and the *why* you identified in Chapter 2.

INSIGHT

"I was tired of being passed over, so I decided to do something about it."

PhD, Social Sciences

Typical resources for part-time and self-funded candidates

A part-time or self-funded doctoral student works on their doctorate under the supervision of a supervisor/promoter within a faculty. Institutions provide resources for registered students. Clarify what resources and benefits are available to you.

Self-funded or part-time candidates, in general, receive:

1. An official university email address and a student number.
2. Library access (both in-person and online access to resources, journals, data bases and the internet).
3. Supervisor support and assistance throughout the doctoral programme.
4. Permission to call themselves a PhD or doctoral candidate on social platforms and in email signatures to facilitate contact with stakeholders, researchers, and institutions who can support doctoral progress.
5. Support from the institution's graduate research department for project or funding applications and questions relating to the programme and standards and regulations.
6. Contact details on the institution's personnel/faculty contact page.
7. Access to the institution's academic repository to upload publications.
8. Access to various courses offered to all PhD candidates to aid progress, support wellbeing, and up-skill.

In general, self-funded candidates have limited or no access to the following:

Self-funded or part-time candidates do not have a designated office space. Some institutional libraries offer limited post-graduate study spaces, while access to facilities such as printers, scanners, or computers may vary.

In general, self-funded candidates do not receive financial support from their institution or their employer to help them complete their studies.

Some institutions provide student accident insurance when you are on-site and public liability insurance relating to research. In general, self-funded candidates are responsible for their healthcare costs.

Self-funded PhD researchers do not have a budget for extra costs incurred on a programme such as fieldwork, events, and specialist facilities. This can limit opportunities to participate in conferences, seminars, or workshops.

Requirements

Self-funded candidates are required to complete the doctoral training programme of their chosen discipline. Self-funded candidates, in general, are exempt from some training requirements of funded peers. They are not obliged to conduct faculty administration, teach, or provide other services.

Depending on the type of doctorate undertaken, most of the following components are compulsory:

1. Write a minimum of one scientific, peer-reviewed, international publication and/or submit a thesis, dissertation or commentary.
2. Organise and deliver a minimum of two peer-to-peer seminars.
3. Complete a minimum of one seminar series specifically for doctoral candidates.
4. Present at least one oral or poster presentation about your doctoral research at an international scholarly conference.
5. Complete research integrity training.
6. Develop a data management plan.
7. Complete and submit an annual progress report to reflect with the supervisor on what stage you are at in your PhD and where it is going.

Key considerations for part-time or self-funded candidates on the demands of a PhD:

It requires self-reliance and the ability to take initiative, plan, structure your work independently, and reach key milestones and deadlines. It is often up to the candidate to proactively engage with your supervisor and seek feedback.

Self-funded and part-time PhD researchers often take between four to seven years to complete their doctorate. The duration and level of commitment required can impact personal wellbeing. Additionally, if the state of the art (the most recent stage in developing a product, incorporating the newest technology, ideas, and features) has moved on, the relevance of the research can diminish.

Funding opportunities may be limited because candidates returning to academia on a part-time basis might not meet eligibility criteria.

INSIDER TIPS

Plan your PhD, the scope of the project, and the time frame to complete it.

Check access to resources, funds, insurance, health benefits, and training.

Clarify additional funding possibilities through the university, your employer, and any tax benefits.

Building a sense of belonging

It can be difficult to experience collegiality or feel part of the faculty or doctoral peer community when on-campus time is constrained by outside work commitments and you have no desk to work from.

Ask your supervisor and the graduate department to connect you with other doctoral students. If there is time, join a student society or network. When possible, attend research meetings, connect with faculty members, and ensure you are on relevant mailing lists, WhatsApp, and social media groups to network and get updates on activities, news, and potential opportunities.

Regularly check university/student email for updates on faculty and on the doctoral programme.

Actions at the start of a doctorate

(0–3 months full-time/0–1 year part-time)

Clear communication and aligning expectations are key requirements for a successful candidate-supervisor relationship for part-time and self-funded candidates.

Within the first three months, organise a right-from-the-start meeting with your supervisor to establish a solid foundation for your work together. Use the meeting to determine working methods, align expectations, and develop a clear road map for the coming years. Establish a realistic meeting schedule and explicitly state who does what and by when. In addition, develop a plan outlining year-one outcomes such as publication planning, conference attendance, chapter deadlines, updates and so on. The meeting should also be used to agree on the first iteration of the research question, the initial approach, and be used to prepare a supervision agreement.

The nature of a part-time doctorate can be a disjointed, fragmented experience. Be realistic about timings and approval times; for instance, it can take six months to a year for a publication to be accepted and certain tasks take longer to complete than expected.

INSIGHT

"Time management is perhaps the most important parameter. When we mean time management, we also mean quality time: if a is task estimated to take, two hours, you need to book a block of at least 2.5–3 hours with no other distractions. You need to immerse in the work, isolate everything else and focus on the task. Trying to work on the task in bursts of 5, 10, 20 minutes and having to do other things in between will take much much longer to complete. The quality of the output will not be as good (if you ever manage to complete)."

Professor, supervisor, Head of Department,
Computer Science

Familiarise yourself with the supports available for part-time, self-funded candidates on practical items such as IT, access to tools, resources, and coaching to aid progress, digital scholarship, and guidance on what to do if you run into problems with your doctorate or supervisor or need to put your PhD on hold for personal or professional reasons.

Developing a research topic

Mature or self-funded candidates, according to interview participants, are more likely to apply for PhD programmes without a defined scope. They engage with a potential supervisor/promoter to identify a research topic. Alternatively, a self-funded candidate can develop a research idea aligned with their interests and then identify an institution and supervisor that can meet their needs by searching through specialist listings for PhDs with similar themes.

Where do I start?

Start by reflecting on what interests you. Examine what is happening in your area to identify gaps in knowledge and potential areas for study. Go deeper and read the latest literature. Research the work of opinion formers, leading scholars, and innovators in the sector. Network and attend conferences. Observe trends and brainstorm potential topics.

Then, a research proposal is developed as part of the application process. Most institutions provide a framework. The proposal contains the project title, the rationale, and the background. In addition, research aims, objectives, and proposed methodology are provided, as well as a timetable for completion, a bibliography, information sources, and an abstract.

Exercise: Where do I start? Develop a draft research proposal

Review the headings below and draft a research proposal for your doctorate. This version is for you, focus on completing the task rather than grammar and syntax. What do you hope to achieve, and how will you do it? Structure the document as follows:

1. Project title
2. Rationale and background
3. Research aims
4. Research objectives
5. The approach used to conduct the research (the methodology)
6. Timetable for completion
7. List of resources used to draft the research proposal

> Important: Proposals evolve. Your idea will adapt, mature, and develop. Be open to feedback and change.

Exercise: Self-reflection on the first draft of the research proposal

As you explore the ideas you are interested in and when an early first version proposal is developing, ask yourself.

1. Is the research proposal understandable and relevant?
2. Is there a need for this knowledge?
3. Am I genuinely interested in this?

4. Am I capable of developing and addressing the research question?
5. Have I set achievable and measurable aims and objectives?
6. Is the time frame and level of commitment realistic?
7. Based on what I know, is the topic original?
8. Does it contribute to new knowledge?
9. Is the rationale clear, objective, and compelling?
10. Does the abstract contain the most important elements of the proposal?
11. Does it meet word count and structure requirements?
12. Is the university the right one (expertise, resources, reputation, and access) so that I successfully complete my studies?

PhD Agreement

In the first three months of a programme, a PhD Agreement form is signed. In general, an agreement contains the following:

1. Working title of the research.
2. Name of supervisor(s) and members of supervisory team.
3. Research description and initial planning.
4. An acceptable project plan and framework for supervision.
5. Estimated timeframes and milestones (specifically stated for years one to two; generally stated for the remainder of the programme years four to seven).
6. Year 1: Doctoral candidates and the supervisors clearly describe the research subject, progress criteria (go/no go), and the responsibilities of all those involved in the PhD Agreement. Project funding agreements are also documented.

Doctoral education planning

Confirm the skills and competencies to be developed and the required courses for the doctoral programme. Doctoral educational training courses aim to develop transferable, research, and discipline-related skills and can be included in annual reviews and in the thesis. The focus is on (research) topic or content-related courses, methods, and methodology-related courses as well as skill development, competency, and career-orientated programmes.

Supervision agreements

Supervision: The academic, or academics, who act as a guide for doctoral candidates.

Formalising the nature of supervision with the supervisory team is a key driver of completion and includes scheduled meetings throughout the programme.

Supervisors ensure that the project's aims, content, and planning for the next four to seven years are realistic and establish the right working conditions for their doctoral candidates. This includes the division of specific responsibilities between the candidate, peers, and the institution.

Education and financial support (if available)

Confirmation of any educational and financial support to attend conferences and meetings or to participate in various research communities and other non-research activities should be included in the PhD agreement. In some situations, a candidate might receive departmental financial support or a research budget to travel and present at international scientific conferences.

INSIDER TIP

Identify the conferences, events, and meetings that can help you progress. Work out the costs and reserve a personal budget if funding support does not materialise.

Balancing work and the doctorate

Mutually agree on the amount of time expected to spend on the doctorate, work, family life, and other activities. Those interviewed for the book indicated that doctoral candidates could expect to spend ten to twenty hours a week on their project. The timing of some activities should be planned so that the risk of delay is minimised.

Data management plan

Data management plan (DMP) guidelines provided by your organisation should be adhered to and follow FAIR (Findable, Accessible, Interoperable, and Reusable) Principles which are used internationally (Wilkinson et al. 2016). Data management plans document the roles and responsibilities of personnel with access to the data – the types of data stored, formats, and metadata. Policies and protocols on access, sharing, privacy, reuse, distribution, and dissemination are given. In addition, data storage, curation, and preservation details are included, and costs are given (see Table 3.2).

In research, the term data refers to the collection of information analysed and used to reach an academic conclusion. This is unique to your faculty and area of research and can include data gathered through observation, experiment, simulation, and data processing.

It is your responsibility as a doctoral candidate to identify any risk relating to privacy, storage of information, permission to use, consent, and ownership. When the research methodology is developed, decisions on data collection, storage, file formats, cyber protection, and backups will emerge and follow conventions in your area of expertise. These decisions and processes are carefully documented in the data management plan. In general, data relating to doctoral work is registered, accurately documented, and safely stored for a minimum of ten years for review when the doctoral research is complete.

TABLE 3.2 Data management plan elements

STEP 1: Reflect on the following

1. Research title and focus of the study
2. Date the plan was created/updated (version number and date)
3. Who has access to the plan and data (identify the names, their roles, and level of access to the data)?
4. Will I use existing data for the research?
5. If I plan to produce new data, what type of data do I expect the research to generate?
6. In what format and volume do I expect data to be collected and/or produced? For instance, databases, spreadsheets, documents, audio, image, video, mixed media. Saved as PDF, excel, text, or in other formats.
7. Is the data open source (open to others for academic purposes)? If not, why not?
8. How will the data and metadata be stored and backed up during and after the programme?
9. How much storage capacity is needed?
10. What data security steps have been taken to protect data, keep information secure and protect sensitive data during and after the doctoral programme?
11. How will I process and store personal data and demonstrate that my research complies with current privacy legislation?
12. How have I clarified who owns that data and any intellectual property rights relating to the work?
13. How will the data be preserved for ten years after the doctoral programme is complete?
14. Are there any legal, privacy, or security reasons to restrict access to the data or not make it available publicly?
15. Will the data be available for reuse? If so, what is available, what are the conditions, and for how long? What repository will be used?
16. Are there plans to disseminate information related to the data and the research findings?
17. What is the cost of resources dedicated to data management to ensure that data is FAIR (Findable, Accessible, Interoperable, Reusable)? Who is responsible for that cost?
18. Who is responsible and liable if data is compromised?

STEP 2: Review and update throughout the doctoral programme

1. Are there any gaps in the data management plan?
2. Does it make sense?
3. How specifically, can you improve content and flow, identify and mitigate potential risks?

Data management plan elements. © 2023 Sinéad Hewson.

Familiarise yourself with data management plan requirements for your programme and document the process. Many institutions provide training workshops and online tools to capture this information.

Although this is time-consuming at the start of the programme and is developed under the supervision of the institution you are in, a well-constructed, future-proof data management plan is a marker of excellence, supports application approvals, and demonstrates that the data you are responsible for is carefully curated and that your work is robust. It also forms part of the content in research-based dissertations when you tell the story of how you examined, formulated, and developed your research findings.

Exercise: Elements of a data management plan

It is prudent to think about specific requirements relating to the body of work you are developing to meet the requirements of a data management plan. Review Table 3.2 and anticipate what you think is necessary to complete your doctorate. Discuss this with your supervisor and graduate department and check against policies and procedures in your institution, workplace (if applicable), and area of expertise. A data management plan is an evolving document. Update on a regular basis and include it as part of your annual review.

Doctoral Education Programme

Doctoral Education Programmes are structured to support the development of transferable, discipline-related, and research skills. Clarify whether credits can be earned through learning on-the-job activities, such as presenting, publishing, and teaching. Discuss this with your supervisor and develop a plan for the duration of your programme.

Review meeting (annual)

A review of progress, performance, and next steps typically occurs in the first six to nine months of a programme and annually thereafter. Feedback on progress, results, performance, and effort is provided. A formal result on progression is called a go/no-go decision or a recommendation to advance, adapt, or abandon the project and the PhD agreement is updated. Scheduling for the dissertation and viva is generally discussed in month 36 (full-time)/ years four to seven (part-time).

Meet peers and join the PhD community

In the early stages of a PhD, networking and interacting with peers and faculty is encouraged. Turn up, introduce yourself to peers, find out about their work, interests and responsibilities, and if appropriate, ask for advice/insights towards completion.

Taking action

Taking action, and understanding what that means in the context of your work builds on the motivation to complete your PhD identified in Chapter 2. Looking at the bigger picture of where I am now and where I want to be from the Pivoting Model will help articulate the actions necessary to reach your goal. Although there are multiple self-help resources in the market, the Pivoting Model is customisable so that you identify resources that are right for you. Block time in the diary, complete the following exercises, and get organised. This approach will help with planning and personal growth, speed up the process, and keep you focused, adaptable, and committed.

A scalable framework is presented alongside practical exercises and tasks to aid the development of a doctoral work plan and embed critical and consequential thinking behaviours. James Clear, author of Atomic Habits, proposes that achieving a goal is about falling in love with systems and goes on to say that individuals "do not rise to the level" of their "goals", they "fall to the level" of their "systems (Clear, 2018)." Planning defines growth, speeds up the process, and keeps you focused, adaptable, and committed. Start by developing a five-minute mock presentation of your research and see what comes up (see Table 3.3).

Exercise: Prepare a 5-minute presentation on your research

This exercise can act as a leveller to redesign the research question, familiarise yourself with the culture you are joining, and start the process of sitting comfortably with your newly acquired identity as a doctoral candidate, scholar, and researcher.

TABLE 3.3 Exercise: Prepare a five-minute presentation of your research

STEP 1: 5-minute presentation

Prepare a 5-minute presentation on your doctorate. It should follow the structure of and answer the following questions:

1. What is your project about? (General description).
2. What exactly are you studying? What are you not examining? (Scope).
3. What is decided? What is still open? (Scope).
4. Where are you now in your project? (General project status update).
5. Focus on the next 12 months, starting today: What will you work/ focus on? What are your general plans/ideas for next year?

STEP 2: Record the presentation

1. Record the presentation as if you are presenting your idea in a virtual meeting (use Zoom, Teams, or an equivalent platform).

STEP 3: Review the recording

1. Are there any gaps?
2. Does it make sense?
3. How, specifically, can you improve content and flow?

Prepare a five-minute presentation of your research. © 2023 Sinéad Hewson.

▶ ACTIONS IN THE MIDDLE OF A DOCTORATE

(4–42 months full-time/2–4 years part-time)

Generally, primary research is conducted at this stage, supervision continues, and annual progress meetings roll on. Important milestones such as the transfer exam* (which is an exam taken to assess whether one can move from one stream of academic study to another) and final progress presentations take place. These assessments are used to calibrate the standard of the work, the current state of the research project, and to check that it meets the standard for a doctoral award. During this time, active participation at conferences, meetings, and peer events is expected and is an opportunity to present the work, secure peer and opinion leader feedback, and test hypotheses as well as evaluate initial research findings.

*A word of caution. The literature suggests that this is the time when part-time dropouts occur. Connecting with your supervisor or engaging with a trusted confidant is invaluable. Adoption of habits such as self-reflection, focus, self-care, learning from setbacks, being open to unexpected results, and knowing when to seek support are critical at this time. Remember WHY you are doing this.

▶ ACTIONS TOWARDS THE END OF A DOCTORATE

(42–48 months full-time/4–7 years part-time)

Preparing to cross the finish line

Graduates describe this part of the doctoral as a transformational process with a significant amount of time working in isolation reflecting on ideas, connecting data and information, and formulating conclusions. Information in the public domain uses phrases such as sacrifice, perseverance, loneliness, and even pain to describe this experience. It is challenging and can push individuals out of their comfort zone writing long-form material for the first time in many years and experiencing vulnerability when the work is out there, for others to see. This phase is an opportunity to immerse yourself in a subject that you are passionate about, analyse data, and express your point of view on a particular issue. It is a springboard to the future you visualised in Chapter 2.

The generic thesis structure and checklist detailed in *Chapter 6: Thesis structure, literature review and checklists* acts as a guide for this part of the doctoral journey. You are seeking the highest academic award for your work, and part of operating at this level is to acknowledge that your work will be examined carefully by peers inside and outside of academia. In every presentation, submission, and meeting expect to be challenged on your assumptions, the literature, methodology and conclusions. That is how it is meant to be. Enjoy the experience and use the latter part of the doctorate to prepare and deliver a thought-provoking dissertation. Plan and prepare well for the defence. Remind yourself why you are putting yourself and your family through this and focus.

Countdown to the dissertation and defence

Chunking the process into key steps makes the process achievable and helps you recognise that the finish line is in sight.

1. Develop a draft version of the dissertation or analysis of the body of work you plan to use for the doctoral defence.
2. Submit a draft version of the document for feedback and comments by your supervisor and promoter.
3. Listen to the feedback, adjust the document, and ensure that your promoter and supervisor confirm in writing that the body of work is approved and suitable for submission for the award of PhD/a doctorate in your specialist area.
4. Check that the correct paperwork, materials, and fees have been submitted on time to secure an invitation to defend your work.

5. Discuss and agree with your supervisor the proposed choice of independent examiner and internal examiner.
6. Confirm the timeline for submission, the defence, final edits, and graduation.
7. Check your work for plagiarism, grammatical and content errors before the plagiarism scan is conducted by the awarding institution or promoter.
8. Finalise the date and prepare for the thesis defence/viva.

Doctoral defence

The viva or thesis defence is the cornerstone of the doctoral experience and an opportunity to demonstrate the quality and robustness of the work amongst peers. In the final stages of the programme, clarify expectations with your supervisor and graduate research department and check the logistics of how these sessions run. Who will attend? The date, time, location, and running order. Is it in person or virtual? Are there guidelines on what to present, document formats, technical setup, and the dress code? Developing content for the viva is discussed in Chapter 11.

Edits and completion

The viva should be seen as an interim step before the doctoral process is complete. It is described as the *cornerstone* of the doctoral experience and an opportunity to demonstrate the quality of you as an academic expert and the robustness of the work.

The majority of vivas end with a recommendation to edit the work and the candidate is presented with a series of edits (called minor edits or major corrections) before the award of doctorate is given. Accept before you enter the room that you will be requested to edit the work and schedule a significant chunk of time to complete the task. Some candidates want to stop as soon as the viva is over, take annual leave, or are already committed to a new project. Set a personal goal to complete minor edits within a month of receiving formal feedback in writing. It is a window of opportunity where you are still engaged with the material, and it is easier to continue rather than refamiliarise yourself with the data after a break of a couple of weeks.

After completion

On completion, some candidates expressed a sense of loss, having lived with the doctorate for four, seven, or even ten years and that it is hard to let go of. Remember to celebrate and take time out to reflect on how you have transformed personally and professionally.

Update your professional and personal profiles. Consider where the body of work, your advanced competencies in critical thinking, analysis, and examination of data can be put to good work and reach a wider audience. Join professional and alumni networks and act as a role model for family, peers, and members of your community.

Be kind to yourself.

▶ TECHNOLOGY

Mastering technology and treating it "as your friend" is critical to the success of *organisation*, the second doctoral completion trigger. Taking a systemic approach, using technology as a knowledge manager, and acting purposefully helps candidates incubate, shape, and sharpen points of view that contribute to the final work. Effective use of technology can channel, capture, organise, and accumulate information, and focus ideas, opinions and arguments. The effort to research and identify appropriate tools to manage accumulated knowledge, archive information, and store references pays off towards the end of a doctorate (see Tables 3.4, 3.5, and 3.6). It is easier for the researcher to make clear associations and identify gaps when formulating academic arguments and transforming abstract ideas into concrete concepts.
When choosing technology tools, consider how you take notes, absorb, and process information. Choosing tools that are fit for

purpose and right for you is important. Personal preference, the type of device, availability on and offline, accessibility, ease of use, price, and recommendations from trusted sources all factor in the final decision. The three exercises that follow will help you focus on what you need (see Tables 3.4, 3.5, and 3.6).

TABLE 3.4 Exercise: Technology I. What are my preferences?

STEP 1: Preference check **Duration:** 10 mins	First of all, reflect on how you take notes, absorb, and process information. Do you prefer to: 1. Use whatever tools are available without really thinking about it. 2. Schedule, create, and customise processes to develop ideas. 3. Reflect, and then connect ideas, patterns, and concepts to formulate ideas. 4. Gather, sort, and categorise information for later use.	
STEP 2: Love/Hate **Duration:** 30–45 mins	Identify five technologies that are invaluable to you/love. For each, write down. 1. Name. 2. How it works/what it does. 3. Why you like it. 4. How it makes life easier. 5. Ways it can be improved. 6. Why you will use it.	Identify five technologies that you dislike. For each, write down. 1. Name. 2. How it works/what it does. 3. Why you dislike it. 4. How it makes life harder. 5. Ways it can be improved. 6. Why you chose not to use it.
STEP 3: Write/ Record **Duration:** 15–30 mins	Summarise: 1. What are the three most useful insights from this task? 2. How will these insights help you with your doctorate?	
I PREFER TO:		

TABLE 3.5 Exercise: Technology II. Recommendations

STEP 1: Technology scan	Reflect on where you are in the doctoral process and identify useful resources to help you complete.
Duration: Varies **Frequency**: Ongoing	1. Seek recommendations and advice on suitable resources and technology from supervisors, faculty, peers, and librarians to get the work done effectively. 2. Engage with peers, other students, school leavers, and online fora, clarify: does the technology or resource work as expected? What would they recommend? 3. Review the technology Is the recommendation valid? Does this technology add value?
STEP 2: Tech review **Duration**: allow 20–45 mins per item **Frequency**: Every 2–3 months	Review potential technology and resources for the programme. For each, write down. 1. Name (product/service) 2. Cost (one-off, monthly, annual, provided by the university) 3. What it does 4. Pros of the product/service 5. Cons of the product/service 6. Source (I already use it, recommended, internet etc.) 7. Does it work across multiple devices and platforms (which ones)? 8. Is it compatible with my current technology setup? 9. Is it compatible with university systems? Is it permitted? 10. In what way can I adapt it to meet my needs? 11. What are the steps required to learn, set up, and adapt for my use? 12. In what way can this resource help me with the doctorate. 13. Is it secure and encrypted? 14. Is it the best use of my time? Is it worth the effort? 15. Reasons to use. 16. Reasons not to use. 17. Decision (yes, no, review at a later date). 18. Who can help me with this?

(*Continued*)

TABLE 3.5 (Continued)

STEP 3: Technology choice **Duration**: 30–60 mins **Frequency**: Every 2–3 months	Reflect on the progression of your doctorate and the expected next steps. If you had to choose three to five critical resources, what would they be? Here are some prompts to get started: Calendar; Conference call/meeting tool; Dictation/note-taking tool; Finance tracker; Health tracker; Journaling tool; Project management; Reading/listening tool; Resource/article/journal storage/citation tool; Writing tool.
STEP 4: Write/Record **Duration**: 15–30 mins	Summarise: 1. What are the three most useful insights from this task? 2. How will these insights help you with your doctorate?

I PREFER TO:

IN WHAT WAY CAN TECHNOLOGY HELP ME COMPLETE MY DOCTORATE?

Pivoting I. Something needs to change. © 2019–2023 Sinéad Hewson.

▶ TECHNOLOGY RESOURCES

Handy tools

The following section references a number of tools which can be used to aid doctoral candidates in organising their work and processing data. This is not an exhaustive list and is structured to prompt thinking on what tools you need to complete your doctoral programme. The third technology exercise takes a pragmatic approach to whether a tool is relevant for the doctoral programme or not (see Table 3.6). Divide your resources into must have, nice to have resources.

Reference management tools

Mendely Reference Manager and **Zotero** are free while **Paperpile** is a paid web and desktop reference management application where users can store, organise, and search for references and take notes. References and bibliographies can also be inserted into documents. They have pretty much replaced **Excel**, which would have been used in the past to store notes and annotate articles.

Note and task-management tools

Evernote and **One Note** are note-taking and task-management applications. Both are used to archive and create searchable, sharable notes. The tools are used to save text, web content, images, audio, and multiple file formats.

Writing tools

Microsoft Word and **Google Docs** are the most widely used tool for academics. They are easy to use and have inbuilt grammar, spelling and accessibility checkers, thesaurus, text formatting and aligning, bullets and numbering, inserting watermarks, page numbers headers and footers, and can be integrated with some citation tools. Microsoft Word was used to format this book. The open source versions of Word are called **Open Office** and **Libre Office**. Documents can be created and edited online with the ability to collaborate with others.

LaTeX is a free programme used to publish scientific papers, theses, and books. Text is submitted in plain text. However, it takes time to learn how to add tags and format text. Built-in features are similar to Microsoft Word as well as the ability to cross-reference materials, bibliography, page layout, chapter and section headings, and numbering. A bibliography and references are automatically generated using BibTeX or BibLaTeX.

Scrivener is a long-form writing tool useful for managing a lengthy document such as a book or a thesis with multiple chapters, sections, and sub-sections. It was used for the development of this book.

Grammarly and **Turnitin** have tools that can check against plagiarism, such as direct copies or use of other people's work without proper attribution, and when blocks of text are mixed and matched from multiple sources. They do not fact-check or show factual errors.

Academic search tools

Google Scholar is a useful tool to initially search for scholarly literature and provides abstract snippets for users. It is currently the most popular academic search tool. While the largest open-access research platform is **CORE**, and PDF formats are provided. Other tools include **BASE** (Bielefeld Academic Search Engine) in Germany while **Science.gov** provides search results from U.S. federal agencies. **Semantic Scholar** uses AI to customise search results and identify connections between research topics. **Baidu Scholar** provides English language and Chinese research papers.

Productivity tools

Focusmate is a collaborative working space with free and paid options. Users partner with another person and commit to complete a piece of work in real-time online in 25-, 50-, or 75-minute time slots. An offline option is to practise the Pomodoro Method by breaking tasks down into chunks of work and using a timer to complete the task within a set time period.

TABLE 3.6 Exercise: Technology III. The technology I need to complete my Doctorate

Name:	**Cost:**

What it does:

Pros:	**Cons:**
1.	1.
2.	2.
3.	3.

Source	**Does it work across multiple**
(I already use it, recommended, internet, etc.)	**devices and platforms** (which ones)?

Is it compatible with my current technology setup?	**Is it compatible with university systems? Is it permitted?**

Ways to adapt to meet my needs.	**Steps required to learn, set up, adapt.**
1.	1.
2.	2.
3.	3.

Ways it can help me with the doctorate.	**Is it secure, encrypted?**

Reasons to use.	**Reasons not to use.**
1.	1.
2.	2.
3.	3.

Decision: (yes, no, review later)	**Who can help me with this?**

Next steps/Date:
1.
2.
3.

ARTIFICIAL INTELLIGENCE

If you choose to use artificial intelligence (AI)/machine learning (ML) resources in the development of ideas, concepts, and resources, please declare this in the same way books, magazines, and information sources are cited by clearly referencing the AI/ML resource name and link in all work/projects submitted.

The European Code of Conduct for Research Integrity recommends that "Researchers report their results and methods, including the use of external services or AI and automated tools, in a way that is compatible with the accepted norms of the discipline and facilitates verification or replication, where applicable." It goes on to say that "hiding the use of AI or automated tools in the creation of content or drafting of publications" is inappropriate (ALLEA, 2023).

For instance, in the final editing stages, I used the reviewing tool in *Microsoft*, *Grammarly*, and the *Magic Write Function on Canva* to support manual proofreading of the material. These tools can check sentence structure, identify alternatives for repeating words and phrases, or check for gaps in an argument and propose an alternative word order. I also ran blocks of text through *Grammarly's* online plagiarism checker. It is a useful way to check for missed quotation marks, citations, or if a piece of text you create appears similar to something already in existence. I used *ChatGPT* as a brainstorming tool to generate alternative book titles using words or phrases from search terms to find books for doctorates, this is because the original title lacked clarity and needed a clear call to action. The tools help spark ideas, but they are neither logical nor intuitive and the quality and accuracy of output varies. The final book title bears no resemblance to the ChatGPT-generated suggestions. Checking AI-generated text takes time, a significant amount of time. AI can help refine or polish text and develop an agenda, but it does not replace original ideas, opinion, fact-based arguments, or words of wisdom (yet). A 70 word sample text follows and you can decide for yourself.

SAMPLE GRAMMARLY EDIT

ORIGINAL: UNEDITED

When I write, my first drafts are verbose, some writers call it the vomit version. I focus on the key points, putting text on the pages. I tested Grammarly to see if it can improve the structure. It can rephrase, adjust the tone, expand, or shorten text. I've written for many years, and at the moment, it takes more effort to check accuracy and for plagiarism. Is it ethical?

REPHRASE FUNCTION

When I begin writing, my initial drafts tend to be lengthy and over-expressive, which some writers refer to as the "vomit version". My primary objective is to get the ideas down on paper. To enhance the structure, I tried out Grammarly and discovered that it can modify the tone, reword sentences, and adjust the length of the text. Despite having years of experience in writing, I find myself exerting more effort to ensure accuracy and avoid plagiarism. Is this ethical?

SHORTEN IT FUNCTION

When I first write, it's usually a long and info-packed "vomit" draft. To fix the structure, I tried using Grammarly. It can rephrase, change tone, and even shorten or expand text. Even with experience, avoiding plagiarism is tough, which raises ethical concerns.

Writing and artificial intelligence

Can AI write the literature review for me? AI can only write and reference what it has been trained to report on. Even though citations and references are included in AI texts, it does not necessarily mean that the citations exist, are accurate, or are relevant to the research topic. At the time of writing, AI is useful as an editing tool, it is maturing and, depending on the area of expertise, checking results can be more time-consuming than doing it yourself.

A word of caution. AI tools are evolving as are the trackers available to detect their use. Some universities and opinion formers report that AI tracking tools have a level of uncertainty in detecting the use of AI-generated work. There have been instances of using spell-check/sense-check functionality to polish text which can incorrectly suggest that material is AI generated.

INSIDER TIPS

Transcripts and technology: Use transcript generators in Zoom or tools such as otter.ai to transcribe interview notes. This frees up time to focus on the content and analyse what is said rather than endless typing.

▶ SUMMARY

To complete a doctorate successfully, organisation is key, and it is your responsibility to understand what is expected of you and others. This chapter outlined the approaches, resources, and requirements to complete a PhD, and getting a grasp of what this means at the start of the process pays off in the final phases because "Well begun is half done".

Topics covered in this chapter are:

Advance, adapt, abandon (go/no go)
Data management plan
Organisation
Own the doctorate
Technology
Typical part-time doctoral journey

▶ USEFUL RESOURCES AND REFERENCES

References

ALLEA - All European Academies. (2017). *The European Code of Conduct for research integrity* (2nd ed., p. 3). Berlin: ALLEA - All European Academies. Available at: https://allea.org/wpcontent/uploads/2017/05/ALLEA-European-Code-of-Conduct-for-Research-Integrity-2017.pdf: ISBN: 978-3-00-055767-5.

ALLEA. (2023). *The European Code of Conduct for research integrity – Revised Edition 2023*. Berlin. doi:10.26356/ECOC: ISBN: 978-3-9823562-3-5.

Clear, J. (2018). *Atomic habits* (p. 27). Random House Business Books, London. Kindle Edition: ISBN: 9781473537804.

Wilkinson, M.D. et al. (2016). The FAIR guiding principles for scientific data management and stewardship, *Scientific Data*, 3, 160018. doi:10.1038/sdata.2016.18 Available at: http://www.nature.com/articles/sdata201618 [Accessed 15 January 2017].

A selection of useful resources

21st Century Doctorate. https://www.qaa.ac.uk/scotland/development-projects/learning-from-international-practice/21st-century-doctorate#

Canva. www.canva.com

Discover PhDs. www.discoverphds.com

Evernote. https://evernote.com/

Excel. https://www.microsoft.com/en-us/microsoft-365/excel

Focusmate. www.focusmate.com

Foster Open Science. https://www.fosteropenscience.eu/

Franklin University. https://www.franklin.edu/degrees/doctoral

Freedom. App. https://freedom.to/

Google. https://www.google.com/docs/about/

Google. https://scholar.google.com/

Grammarly. https://www.grammarly.com/proofreading

KU Leuven. https://research.kuleuven.be/en/career/phd

LaTeX. https://www.latex-project.org/

Libre Office. https://www.libreoffice.org/

Magic write (see Canva). https://www.canva.com/magic-write/

Mendeley https://www.mendeley.com/

Microsoft Word. https://www.microsoft.com/en-us/microsoft-365/word

Miro (app). https://miro.com/

OneNote.https://www.microsoft.com/en-us/microsoft-365/onenote/digital-note-taking-app

Open Office. https://www.openoffice.org/

Paperpile. https://paperpile.com/

Scrivener. https://www.literatureandlatte.com/scrivener/overview

Semantic. https://www.semanticscholar.org/

TU Delft PhD Guidelines Guide for Doctoral Candidates and Supervisors. https://filelist.tudelft.nl/3mE/Onderzoek/Graduate%20School/PhD-Guidebook_web.pdf

TU Dublin Graduate Research Regulations. https://www.tudublin.ie/media/website/research/postgraduate-research/graduate-research-school/documents/Graduate-Research-Regulations-1st-Edition.pdf

Zoom. https://zoom.us/

4 Planning and project management

▶ INTRODUCTION

Doctoral Learning Outcomes presented at the start of the book (Table 1.1) highlight that PhD candidates must demonstrate (i) knowledge and understanding of their specialist area, (ii) the proficiency and the ability to design, plan, and conduct research with rigour and (iii) solid judgement and approach to act with intellectual independence and integrity. Completion depends on understanding the process, which was discussed using the Scalable part-time Doctoral Framework (Figure 3.1) as a point of reference. The Planning and project management chapter expands on this with useful exercises and tasks that aim to help users develop a practical, achievable work plan embedded with critical and consequential thinking behaviours (see Tables 4.1, 4.2, 4.3, and 4.4). There are useful questions and checklists to help you move towards completion and adapt these frameworks to meet your

DOI: 10.4324/9781003413691-6

needs or use them as prompts. The original versions of these checklists were developed to support my own needs as a novice academic to unpick the research process and align it with research integrity standards. They have been updated based on the literature and discussions with mature masters and PhD candidates and peers. Focus on what is relevant for your doctoral journey and take care to follow the guidelines of your institution closely. "Own your doctorate".

The chapter closes with a summary of key concepts and recommended exercises and introduces the theme of *Chapter 5: Research and critical thinking.*

▶ PROJECT MANAGEMENT. OWN YOUR DOCTORATE

Exercise: Pivoting IV. What are my challenges?

At the start of the doctoral process, acknowledging challenges that can enable or hinder completion, creates an opportunity to plan and establish clear ways of working to complete tasks.

Before you start, spend 15–30 minutes reacquainting yourself with the contents of the Scalable part-time Doctoral Framework (Figure 3.1), the customised version you created (Exercise: My Doctoral Framework), and the Generic doctoral/PhD Timeline (Table 3.1). Take a blank sheet of paper and complete the exercises called Pivoting VI. What are my challenges? (Table 4.1), Pivoting VII. How will I know I have reached my goal? (Table 4.2), and Pivoting VIII. What if? (Table 4.3).

Complete this exercise in a space where you can focus, think clearly, and won't get disturbed by others. Notice what comes up.

For a guided audio, go to the resources page of www.unconventionaldoctorates.com

TABLE 4.1 Exercise: Pivoting VI. What are my challenges?

STEP 1: Reality check	Reflect on the following:
Duration: 45 mins	1. Write down all of your challenges on a blank page, post-its, or whiteboard. Include everything that springs to mind relating to you, family, work resources etc. 2. Cluster them into similar themes or packages. 3. Is there a pattern? Which ones dominate? 4. Describe the challenge in one sentence. 5. Is there a challenge which, if it was addressed, could resolve some smaller challenges at the same time? 6. Which challenge is my Number One Challenge?
STEP 2: Mindset	Identify
Duration: 15–30 mins	1. The three most useful insights from this task. 2. How will the insights help me with my doctorate?
STEP 3: Action	Summarise:
Duration: 15–30 mins	1. Three actions I need to take and by when.

MY CHALLENGES ARE:

MY NUMBER ONE CHALLENGE IS:

Exercise: Pivoting VII. How will I know I have reached my goal?

Complete the exercise, write your immediate, unfiltered responses.

For a guided audio, go to the resources page of www.unconven tionaldoctorates.com

TABLE 4.2 Exercise: Pivoting VII. How will I know I have reached my goal?

STEP 1: **Reality check** **Duration:** 15 mins	Reflect and write down answers to these questions. 1. How will I know I have reached my goal? 2. When you have reached your goal, what will it look like, taste like, and feel like? 3. What will be different? 4. What are the payoffs and benefits of this change?
STEP 2: **Action** **Duration:** 30–45 mins	Focus and document how you are going to do reach your goal. 1. How will I reach my goal? 2. Alone? With others? Who specifically? 3. What support do I have in place? What do I need? 4. When? How do I want this? 5. What resources do I have, and what do I need? 6. Reflect on the three most useful insights from the task. 7. How will the insights help me with my doctorate?
STEP 3: **Action** **Duration:** 15–30 mins	Summarise: Three actions I need to take. Identify the resources and support I need and by when.

IN WHAT WAY CAN THIS EXERCISE HELP ME COMPLETE MY DOCTORATE?

Exercise: Pivoting VIII. What if?

Complete the exercise, write your immediate, unfiltered responses.

For a guided audio, go to the resources page of www.unconven tionaldoctorates.com

TABLE 4.3 Exercise: Pivoting VIII. What if?

STEP 1: **Why** **Duration**: 10 mins	1. Think about your doctorate and write the first thing that springs to mind. 2. What is your goal?
STEP 2: **Mindset** **Duration**: 15–30 mins	1. What will happen if you achieve your goal? 2. What won't happen if you achieve your goal? 3. What will happen if you do not achieve your goal? 4. What won't happen if you do not achieve your goal? 5. List the three most useful insights from this task. 6. How will the insights help me with my doctorate?
STEP 3: **Action** **Duration**: 15–30 mins	Summarise: Three actions I need to take. Resources and support I need and by when.

What did I gain from the exercise?

Pivoting VIII. What if? © 2023 Sinéad Hewson.

Mindset and project management

> ### INSIGHT
>
> "Completing the PhD was not difficult. I was clear on my goal."
>
> Part-time PhD by prior publication

A growth mindset is the belief that people can develop their abilities, and it is fostered through hard work, strategies, focus, and perseverance. There is a requirement on many institutional programmes to adopt a growth mindset to enable curiosity, deep thinking, and critical analysis and contribute to scholarly discourse. A fixed mindset also has a place at the table because, says Dweck (2017), "there are no great achievements without setbacks". The question for doctoral candidates is how to "persuade our fixed mindset persona to get on board with goals that spring from our growth mindset".

In Chapter 7, Progress, mindsets, and momentum, there is an opportunity to identify moments when you hear your limiting mindset voice stopping you in your tracks and how you can use it to your advantage.

▶ PLANNING

Planning gives clarity and gets ideas down on the page. It makes goals tangible, gives them focus, and helps you prioritise. Effective planning allows you to track progress and make adjustments. In the interviews, participants said that knowing how far you progress keeps you motivated. Taking time to work out what is expected by whom and by when increases completion rate potential.

This section allows you to work out how you will complete the requirements of the doctoral programme (Table 4.4) and create new knowledge along the way. Adapt the content to meet your planning needs.

Exercise: Right from the start. Early-stage planning

INSIDER TIP

Plan early; plan often.

In this exercise, your aim is to define the nature of the doctoral project and estimate the resources, time, and level of input necessary to complete. Find a place where you won't be disturbed for about three hours and document your responses. Repeat every three to six months or as needed throughout the programme. Refer back to the sections on actions at the start, middle, and end of a doctorate in Chapter 3.

When the goal is broken down into smaller chunks, it allows you to list the tasks and estimate the time and costs to complete. Draft an outline or network diagram which maps the project from the start until completion.

Reflect on the structure and adjust the work packages and tasks as necessary. Consider whether the project needs to be scaled downwards to meet current resources or needs an injection of cash, people, or resources to be viable.

Then a step-by-step critical path is developed (captured in a Gantt chart) and resource planning across all areas of responsibility can be estimated. Reflect on and identify the risks (what could go wrong) related to the project and the mitigation measures necessary to address them (i.e. ways to remove, reduce, or manage the risk).

There are some online tools available, such as the planners at www.ithinkwell.com.au and a PhD project management tool at www.klaarinvierjaar.nl which contains icons and tips specific to the doctoral process and has an accompanying book called Project Management for PhDs, which tackles the subject in more detail and is orientated towards full-time candidates (De Bruin & Hertz, 2017).

In Part III, Progress, there is a discussion on what happens when you commence the project. How do you monitor progress, complete tasks, and stay on track? How might you monitor finances and resources against progress? What are the consequences if you need to reschedule if needed? Do you ask for more money, more

TABLE 4.4 Exercise: Right from the start. Early-stage planning

Step 1:

What are the project's goals between now and the end of the doctorate?

Step 2:

1. Chunk down the main goal into a series of intermediate goals to achieve throughout the project.
2. What are they?
3. What is the deadline?

Step 3:

1. Break down the intermediate and primary goals into work packages (WPs).

Step 4:

1. What is the timing of the work packages?
2. When do they start?
3. When do they end?

Step 5:

1. Check the logic and order of WPs.
2. Do they make sense?
3. Adapt as necessary.

Step 6:

1. Estimate costs and resources necessary to complete the project.
2. Adjust as needed.

Adapted from multiple sources, including TU Delft PhD Guidelines; KU Leuven information for PhDs; TU Dublin research graduate Handbook; Franklin University information site for doctorates; UCAS (UK).

help or more time? What is going well, not so well and does something need to change? Complete and review (good, bad, better, do differently).

Sprint

The literature and interviews indicate that in order to progress, completing smaller chunks of work to reach a goal is recommended for PhD candidates. In fact, agile project management methods are best suited for PhD research projects because they prioritise scope delivery.

A selection of doctoral project panagement tips follow:

INSIDER TIP

Take responsibility for the programme. Own the work, own the process, own the ideas, own the thesis.

"Be proactive ... Don't ask to be spoon-fed."

Part-time PhD, Entrepreneurship

▶ WORDS OF ADVICE

At the start of the doctorate

\# 1. **Know thy self**: The closing statement of TU Delft's PhD handbook says "Strength lies in knowing oneself". When you have an idea of the project scale you are undertaking, revisit the exercise you completed on motivation. Ask: Why do I want this, and do the daily tasks align with your personal values and skill set?

\# 2. **Where to start?** Start researching the topic and take notes of what you find. The details will come later. It is useful to begin identifying the most important names, textbooks, and the most cited articles, it will give you a feel for the current state of the art.

\# 3. **Own the doctorate. Know the process, guidelines, expectations, and terminology**: Familiarise yourself with the university guidelines and understand what is expected of you. Identify and understand the terminology and key milestones for the doctorate. Treat the PhD as a long-term project and know where you are on the journey.

4. **Credit for work already completed**: Explore ways to be credited for an existing publication record, work already completed, and prior education.

5. **Resources**: Understand how to access library resources, articles, the internet, and the efficient use of search engines.

6. **Get organised**: Chunk down the work. Identify steps, section by section. Set a deadline – diary time. Stick to the deadline (Allen, 2002; Clear, 2018).

7. **Diary your time**: Fit the doctorate around your work and family. Use the commute (if you have one) to plan regular chunks of time to plan, read, write, and complete chunks of work. Did I say stick to the deadline?

8. **Build the reference database early**: Quickly note where and when you found an article and why you think it is useful. Save your notes in a dedicated article/resources folder on (Excel sheet, Evernote, Mendeley etc.) and include links to the article, uploads, citation, and the document object identifier (DOI) link. When you have time to read the article in detail, build on your notes and update the entry. In your opinion, where might it fit within the dissertation?

9. **Set up a simple searchable system to connect information**: Set up a simple files and folders system, for example, into project, task, action items, and an archive. Be consistent when naming files, folders, and documents. Use tags to link items and references together. Establishing and adapting your filing system allows you to connect ideas and bundles of information (Forte, 2023).

10. **Naming taxonomy**: Be consistent with your naming taxonomy, for example, YY:MM:DD: topic and area of interest. Consistency pays off in the long run, especially when the same format is adopted across different technologies, platforms, and documents. Find a format and structure to meet your needs. For instance, when I travel, I might read something of interest online and then insert a tag or a note in an article that I cannot file yet or email it to myself. If it

is not filed, and search by using the tag or key phrase to find the item almost instantly.

#11. **Retain and archive old material:** Information in electronic form can be retained for later use or as material in a future article. Set up an archive file. In practice, I review my files across platforms every two to four weeks. The items are quickly tagged, kept, adapted, or archived.

Throughout the doctorate

1. **Ask: what is the best use of my time today, at this meeting, with this task?** At the start of the day, ask what the best use is of my (and my team's) time today. What is the most important thing to achieve? Are the opportunities for learning, growth and development? What must I do today to maintain that growth and move closer to completing my doctorate?

2. **Perfect posture:** Be aware of posture, how sit at your desk, and wrist alignment. If you are writing for long periods of time, move, stretch, and step away from the computer every 50–60 mins.

3. **Eyeglasses:** Set up an appointment and check that they are fit for purpose.

Desk/home office set-up

Completing a PhD requires deskwork, and a considerable amount of desk time is spent at the computer conducting research, analysing data, writing, and proofreading. Aim to set up a workspace[1] that is comfortable and supports your needs. Some institutions request that candidates spend time on campus and have dedicated areas or shared spaces where postgraduate candidates can work. There can be times during a doctoral programme when the home environment, work, or the institution itself is not conducive to productivity, and it is useful to explore alternatives.

> "Internet access at home was unstable so I spent chunks of time in the library for desk research and writing. There was too much background noise when I conducted one-to-one interviews by phone, and to overcome this, I accessed a small business workspace for three months. It had stable internet access, a sound-proofed area for conference calls, a secure storage area for files and great coffee. I finally had space to focus and think. It was worth every cent."
>
> Part-time candidate, freelancer

If you have the space at home or another location, find a dedicated space and work surface where you can work, file, easily access information, and think. Use existing equipment, furniture, and lighting. Carefully consider purchases or second-hand items that optimise the space so that the focus is the doctoral work rather than dealing with something niggly like an uncomfortable chair, wobbly tabletop, awkward access to a plug, a printer that does not work, and/or filing mixed with household affairs. Many universities have resources to help you assess your needs.

Stay healthy and move around the workspace to stay energised. Stretch regularly, paying special attention to the spine, arms, wrists, fingers, and neck. Get up, walk, and move throughout the workday. Ensure the room is well-ventilated, drink lots of water, and do some work standing up. While you're seated, stretch your hands, fingers, and arms from time to time.

▶ SUMMARY

The takeaways from this chapter are to treat the doctoral process as a project with a start, a middle, and an end. Organisation is key, and it is your responsibility to own it. Set up a dedicated workspace, and ensure you have access to equipment and resources to complete in a timely fashion. Chunk the work into manageable tasks and dedicate blocks of time where you will be not disturbed to get the work done, to reflect and think deeply.

Topics covered in this chapter are:

Organisation
Own the doctorate
Prioritisation and time management
Project management
Typical part-time doctoral journey

Note

1 IMPORTANT: The information on ergonomic ergometric worksta-
tion set-up is for education purposes only. It does not constitute legal
or professional advice on behalf of the author or publisher. Follow the
guidelines set by your institution or employer and if necessary, seek
professional advice on ways to improve the set-up of your workspace.

▶ USEFUL RESOURCES AND REFERENCES

References

Allen, D. (2002). *Getting things done.* New York. Piatkus Books: ISB:
9780142000281, 9780142000281

Clear, J. (2018). *Atomic habits* (p. 27). Random House. Kindle Edition:
ISBN: 9781473537804.

De Bruin, J., & Hertz, B. (2017). *Project management for PhDs* (2nd ed.).
Amsterdam: Hertz en Boom Uitgevers: ISBN 9789024407101, ISBN
9789024407118.

Dweck, C. S. (2017). *Mindset - Updated edition: Changing the way you
think to fulfil your potential* (p. 260). London: Little, Brown Book
Group: Kindle Edition ISBN: 978-1-47213-996-2.

Forte, T. (2023). *The PARA method.* London: Profile Books Limited: ISBN
978 10081 9542, eISBN 978 10081 9559.

Resources

21st Century Doctorate. https://www.qaa.ac.uk/scotland/development-
projects/learning-from-international-practice/21st-century-
doctorate

Academiac.net. https://academiac.net/2018/10/23/are-gantt-charts-
useful-for-phd-students/

Discover PhDs. www.discoverphds.com

Ergonomics UCLA 4 Steps to Set Up Your Workstation | https://ergonomics.ucla.edu/office-ergonomics/4-steps-set-your-workstation

Ithinkwell.com.au.   https://www.ithinkwell.com.au/index.php?route=product/category&path=78_79_80

KU Leuven. https://research.kuleuven.be/en/career/phd

Project Management for PhDs. https://klaarinvierjaar.nl/

5

Research and critical thinking

INSIGHT

"[One] issue that keeps appearing fairly consistently is the misconception and unpreparedness of the actual research methodology to be followed. PhD students, no matter their experience and age, seem to lack solid competencies of research methods, especially the differences between qualitative and quantitative research. Just by placing a number on an observed phenomenon or item does not mean that this is now quantitative!!!"

Professor, supervisor, Head of Department,
Computer Science

▶ INTRODUCTION

The discussion in this chapter on research and critical thinking prompts PhD candidates to define and identify the research topic and consider ways that a topic can be examined so that the process of

DOI: 10.4324/9781003413691-7

gathering information, analysing data, and articulating results can be synthesised into a superb body of work that contributes to scholarly discourse.

Essential research skills such as curiosity, critical thinking, open-mindedness, and the ability to understand different points of view are the core of doctoral PLGs (Table 1.1.) and are discussed in the chapter. From a research perspective, doctoral candidates must demonstrate proficiency and ability to:

1. Identify and formulate research questions critically, objectively, and creatively.
2. Design, plan, and conduct research, adopting appropriate methods with scientific rigour.
3. Make a significant contribution to the development of knowledge by completing a substantial project and (depending on the type of doctorate) write a thesis and/or several academic articles or a commentary on a prior publication/portfolio.
4. Review and evaluate the work and articulate the findings.
5. Present work logically and coherently following international codes of practice.

Design the Right Thing, the first element of the Scalable Doctoral Framework (Figure 3.1), is used to help candidates explore their area of expertise and develop a research question and methodology which acts as a signpost to conduct the research and complete the work. Then, there is a discussion on the review of the literature and current state of the art, which lays the foundation for the design of the research.

The key takeaways from this chapter are for the reader to know where to start and begin to build a picture of what the research could look like. Designing the research methodology is a time of learning, self-reflection, and growth as a researcher. There will be feedback, and the direction of your study will mature. This is not a moment of failure, it is a moment of growth. Learn, understand, and be open to change.

▶ RESEARCH

INSIDER TIP

In the early to middle stages of the doctorate, you will invest resources to address the doctoral research topic by identifying the research "methods and techniques most useful to the problems at hand" (Trow, 1957; Becker & Geer, 1958; Gill & Johnson, 2002). "Research is the quest for knowledge obtained through systematic study and thinking, observation and experimentation" and you will be tasked with arguing the case for and against using qualitative or quantitative research, or a mix of both to achieve your research goals (ALLEA – All European Academies, 2017).

(see Table 5.1)

Qualitative, quantitative, and mixed methods

As the work matures, the relevance of specific data sets to address the research question and suitable ways to present the material will shift. In general, doctorates present "key findings in context" and as a "logical series of breakdowns" to facilitate analysis discussion and highlight important research points without "overwhelming" the reader. Furthermore, identifying display formats appropriate to the purpose of the study sheds light on how much data should be reported and summarised without changing its nature and meaning. This step also acts as a signpost for the placement of information in the dissertation, whether something remains within a chapter, as an appendix, or is excluded from the thesis.

The following sections build on the exercise, Where do I start? Develop a draft research proposal in Chapter 3 and focus on the Design the Right Thing part of the Scalable part-time Doctoral Framework (Figure 3.1). Refer to them as you answer the questions in this chapter. This section presents a series of reflective questions in plain

TABLE 5.1 Qualitative, quantitative, and mixed methods research

Type	Qualitative	Quantitative	Mixed Methods
Purpose	Understand a problem, context, experience, or issue through observation and/or interview.	Understand the relationship between a number of variables by testing a hypothesis.	Understand the relationship between a number of variables by testing a hypothesis.
Focus	Observe and interpret.	Measure and test.	Both.
	Experience, observation, behaviours, insights.	Numerical, measurable data.	Combines numerical, measurable data with Experience, observation, behaviours, and insights.
	The why behind a behaviour, experience, or context.	The what or how of a behaviour, experience, or context. Proves or disproves something.	The how, what, and why of a behaviour, experience, or context.
Methods	Case study, phenomenological, historical, narrative, preparatory, grounded theory.	Comparative, experimental, exploratory, developmental.	A mixture of methods to examine the research question. Emergent.
Data	Interviews, focus groups, observation, documents, personal accounts, personal papers, records.	Surveys, questionnaires, tests, database reports.	A mixture of interviews, observation, focus groups, surveys, questionnaires, or tests.
Sample collection	Focused. Inclusion/ exclusion criteria.	Random. Inclusion/ exclusion criteria.	Both.
Analysis	Group common data into themes, patterns, clusters.	Statistical analysis.	A combination of both.
Output	Findings, reports, conclusions, and recommendations		

McCloud, S. (2023). Qualitative versus quantitative research methods and data analysis, simply psychology. Stevenson University Library (2023) Research Tips.

English to help readers document key points and identify what is needed to progress and contribute new knowledge. Co-creation, dialogue, and feedback will help you design a robust research approach. Discuss the research question and methodology with your supervisor, clearly state the case for the choices you make, and adapt language to meet the reporting requirements of your institution.

Design the right thing

Identify the doctoral topic/the research question

This reflection builds on the completed exercise Where do I Start? Develop a research proposal and Self-reflection from Chapter 3.

Ask:

1. What specifically is the research problem you want to address?
2. What is the purpose and content of the study?
3. Why is the doctoral study important (to me and for the sector)?
4. Does the research question clearly convey what you hope to achieve?
5. What changes specifically can I make to improve it?/Is it good enough as is?

Literature review/context review/secondary research

Throughout the doctoral programme, you will review the literature and examine the current state of the art. Over time, a list of resources, literature and a knowledge base will emerge that can help you refine your research topic, identify gaps, and articulate why the research deserves a place in academia. The academic material informs the content of the literature review, which is discussed further in Chapter 6 (Thesis structure, literature review, and checklists).

Ask:

1. Can I provide an overview of current scholarly knowledge (theories, models, and concepts)? What specifically will be my focus? What are the criteria for citing this information?
2. Have I identified where the study sits within the academic/sectoral landscape? What are the important points I need to make? Are there gaps or areas of uncertainty that/I need to include?
3. Identify where the study sits within the academic/sectoral landscape.
4. Can I identify gaps, problems, or areas of debate with the current knowledge? In what ways specifically can a study address that gap?
5. What are the most important aspects of a theoretical or conceptual framework that need to be considered? In what way specifically can they guide the research and help later in the process to analyse and synthesise the findings?
6. Can I articulate the research aims or list a series of objectives for the research? What exactly do I want to achieve?

Methodology (rationale)

Unpick and explain your approach. Ask:

1. Can I describe the methodology (the approach) used to address the research question/hypothesis?
2. Does it follow a particular tradition (research type)?
3. Is this approach evidenced, justified, and clear?
4. In what way specifically can I justify the rationale and reasoning for that approach?
5. Are the research context, sample, and inclusion criteria clearly described?
6. Are the data collection and analysis methods clearly presented?

7. What are the specific details of the study design, procedures, and policies (consent, data protection, confidentiality, inclusion/exclusion criteria, do no harm principle, research integrity guidelines, etc.)?
8. Have I explained whether it is a qualitative, quantitative, or mixed methods study? Have I explained why this option has been chosen?
9. Is the approach transparent, trustworthy, and ethical?
10. Is the approach replicable? Does it follow an existing protocol?
11. Are there appropriate safeguards in place for the health, safety, and welfare of me, my institution, peers, and research participants and subjects? What specifically are they?
12. Is this the most suitable methodology to research this particular topic? Why specifically?
13. Is it of a high enough standard to demonstrate my knowledge of research theory and my expertise in the sector?

Primary research/Collect the data

1. What type of data/information is collected? Who, when, where, and why?
2. How will it be stored?
3. Who will have access to it and why?
4. How will it be processed for use later in the study?
5. In the future, can other researchers access and use this data?
6. Does it follow FAIR principles for scientific research (Findable, Accessible, Interoperability, Reusable)? How specifically does it achieve this?
7. Does it align with the research question and the methodology?
8. Who owns the data?

Examine the data. Cluster into themes

1. What techniques do I plan to use and why?
2. Can I compare these themes with other studies?
3. What am I looking for and why?

4. Are there skills I need to develop to complete this task? What are they?
5. Do I have the appropriate resources to complete the task?

Formulate the findings

1. In what way specifically will the findings be reported?
2. How much detail is expected?
3. What techniques do I plan to use and why?
4. Can I compare the findings with other studies?
5. How will I address unexpected/incomplete findings?
6. Do I have the right information to tell the story of the research?
7. Are there skills I need to develop to complete this task? What are they?
8. Do I have the appropriate resources to complete the task?

Analyse and synthesise. Implications and results

1. What way specifically Can I clearly identify patterns, themes, and insights that emerge from the findings?
2. What steps must I take to compare and contrast the findings across themes, context framework, and against existing work?
3. Is the discussion on the meaning and implications of the findings clear? What is missing? What should be removed?
4. Does the analysis demonstrate a deep understanding of the work and its potential to contribute to new knowledge? How, specifically?
5. In what way do the results position the doctoral study as a unique and original piece of work?

Design things right

Test, iterate, validate results

1. In what way specifically can I validate results?
2. Are they reliable and repeatable?

3. Do the results align with FAIR principles? In what way specifically?

The remainder of the Design Things Right part of the Scalable part-time Doctoral Framework is discussed elsewhere in the book. Writing up findings, recommendations, and conclusions are elaborated on in Chapters 6 and 8. Progression milestones such as the annual review, transfer exam, and viva are discussed in Chapters 3 and 11.

Research integrity

Research integrity means conducting research in a way which allows others to have trust and confidence in the methods used and the findings that result from this. The basic principles of research integrity are honesty, responsibility, fairness, and accountability (see Table 5.2). As you review the rules and regulations to conduct research in your institution, consider these as enablers to make your work stronger, more robust, and defendable in the future should someone challenge your ideas at a later date.

It is underpinned by good research practices, which include establishing a good research environment and access to training, supervision, and mentoring. The establishment and practice of good research procedures. Having safeguards in place, robust data practices, and management. It also includes creating opportunities for collaborative working, publication, dissemination, and authorship, and the implementation of credible review and assessment processes. This should be demonstrated in the ways of working within your institution and in the implementation and output of your research. More information can be found in your own institution and on dedicated research integrity platforms such as the Declaration on the Embassy of Good Science (Embassy of Good Science 2022).

TABLE 5.2 Research integrity principles

Principle	Description
Reliability	Reliability ensuring the quality of research, reflected in the design, methodology, analysis, and use of resources.
Honesty	Honesty in developing, undertaking, reviewing, reporting, and communicating research in a transparent, fair, full, and unbiased way.
Respect	Respect for colleagues, research participants, research subjects, society, ecosystems, cultural heritage, and the environment.
Accountability	Accountability for the research from idea to publication, for its management and organisation, for training, supervision, and mentoring, and its wider societal impacts.

ALLEA (2023). The European Code of Conduct for research integrity – revised edition 2023. Berlin. doi:10.26356/ECOC; ISBN: 978-3-9823562-3-5.

Useful research strategies

INSIDER TIPS

Take notes to *record experience*. Don't rely on your memory. Document key points and write something about it.

Summarise and clarify. Write clear notes and simple summaries of articles, meetings, conversations, networking, and items of interest relating to the doctorate. State why it is relevant for the doctorate. Be concise and write something about the (experience, item, data, article, etc.). Summarise an item/article, focus on key points and link pieces of information so that you get a meaningful picture of the research and can use it at a later date.

Search. Understand how to search effectively using keywords, and how to access resources to verify information, data, and claims.

INSIDER TIPS

To make sense of data and information. Read and write to help you focus on the topic. Link pieces of information to get a meaningful picture of the research (Denscombe, 1998).

Retain, archive, delete. Be accurate, and keep sentences short, sharp, and to the point. Ensure content is relevant to the research topic. Ask: Is this information essential or nice to have? Be ruthless and retain the essential "must have" material. Digitally archive "nice to have information" for use at a later stage (Forte, 2023).

Helpful research terminology

Academic approval process: The academic approval process ensures that you're studying units that fit into your course requirements and that you can continue to progress successfully through your studies.

Conflict of interest: A conflict of interest occurs when an individual's personal or professional interests could potentially compromise their impartiality, judgement, decisions, or actions.

Consent: In research, informed consent means that human participants voluntarily participate in research, fully understanding what it means to participate. They give consent before they enter the research.

Declaration of interests: An official statement confirming that you do have (or are not aware of) a connection with someone or something that could impact the perception of your independence and objectivity when making a decision or judgement involving them.

Documentation: In a PhD it is material that provides official information or evidence, or that serves as a record and/or is the process of classifying and annotating text, data, information, etc.

Ethics: moral principles that govern a person's behaviour or the conducting of an activity. The branch of knowledge that deals with moral principles.

Logical fallacies are errors in reasoning that make your argument less effective and convincing. They are expanded on in the discussion on writing.

Referencing (citations) is how you acknowledge the sources of the information you have used (referred to) in your work. It helps to make clear to the reader how you have used the work of others to develop your own ideas and arguments.

Trustworthiness: Trustworthiness or rigour of a study refers to the degree of confidence in data, interpretation, and methods used to ensure the quality of a study (Polit & Beck, 2013).

▶ CRITICAL THINKING

INSIDER TIPS

Curiosity and creativity: Be open to challenges, new ideas, and the unexpected. Brainstorm and notice what appears, question it, and remain curious.

Map and connect: To investigate a topic, map out insights, connect ideas, points of difference, and stakeholder viewpoints. Examine the work from different points of view (perceptual positions) to go deeper into a topic. Brainstorm and consider your study from different perspectives (Dey, 1993).

Critical thinking is the intellectual ability to logically question, analyse, and synthesise assumptions, common beliefs, authority, and explanations and form them into a judgement or next step. Socrates argued that it is important to be able to reflect, question, seek evidence, probe, and consider consequences before an idea is adopted or believed.

For doctoral candidates, this means being open-minded, flexible, and willing to be challenged, combined with the ability to understand different points of view. This also requires a certain amount of scepticism to ask whether something is true, plausible, or simply not valid. Critical thinkers develop well-thought-through arguments built on a foundation of systemic thinking, reasoning, cross-examination, accuracy, and validation of facts. It allows you to think about thinking, think independently, and solve problems.

For example, when analysing data, reading material for a literature review, or any other purpose, ensure that you question the objectives, intent, sources of information, and methods used to gather information. Reflect on the reasoning, how it was reached, and assumptions and implications concerning the work.

To flesh out ideas: Sometimes, you feel that you might have a brilliant idea. Go further, develop it, and brainstorm about it. Formulate ways to make it real and ask yourself what you need to realise it.

Expand ideas and arguments: When an idea or topic sparks curiosity or leads to a potential new idea, expand on it. Ask what is necessary to bring it to fruition.

Exercise: Connect back to the why

Reflect on the research question, the methodology and the purpose of the research. Is the research project motivating you? Does it fulfil the "why am I doing this?" driver identified Part I: Motivation? What changes (if any) will you propose to align the project with your values? What needs to change, you or the research direction? In what ways can I demonstrate excellence through the research?

Exercise: Integrate into the work plan

Review the research plan and break down the work into smaller tasks. Allocate blocks of time to complete the tasks, bit by bit. Integrate this into your workplan.

Reflect: have I taken a SMART (specific, measurable, realistic, and timely) approach to the work? Commit and allocate (undisturbed) time in your agenda to complete the work. Keep it simple and include breaks and time to reflect on the research itself.

▶ SUMMARY

The takeaways from this chapter are to treat the doctoral process as a project with a start, a middle, and an end. Organisation is key, and your responsibility is to understand what is expected of you and others. Set up a dedicated workspace, and ensure you have access to equipment and resources to complete in a timely fashion. Divide the work into manageable tasks and dedicate blocks of time where you will be not disturbed to get the work done, to reflect and think deeply.

Topics covered in this chapter are:

Critical thinking
Methodology
Design things right
Design the right thing
Research question/hypothesis
Research integrity
FAIR principles

▶ USEFUL RESOURCES AND REFERENCES

References

ALLEA - All European Academies. (2017) *The European Code of Conduct for research integrity* (2nd ed., p. 3) Berlin: ALLEA - All European Academies. Available at: https://allea.org/wpcontent/uploads/2017/05/ALLEA-European-Code-of-Conduct-for-Research-Integrity-2017.pdf: ISBN 978-3-00-055767-5.

ALLEA. (2023). *The European Code of Conduct for research integrity – Revised Edition 2023*. Berlin. doi:10.26356/ECOC; ISBN: 978-3-9823562-3-5.

Becker, H., & Geer, B. (1958). "Participant observation and interviewing": A rejoinder. *Human Organization, 17* (2), 39–40. doi:10.17730/humo.17.2.mm7q44u54l347521

Creswell, J. (2002). *Educational research: Planning, conducting, and evaluating quantitative and qualitative research*. Upper Saddle River, NJ: Merrill Prentice Hall: ISBN: 0130917281, 9780130917287.

Declaration: Embassy of Good Science. (2022). https://embassy.science/wiki-wiki/index.php/wiki-wiki/images/f/ff/The-Embassy-of-Good-Science-Declaration.pdf

Denscombe, M. (1998). *The good research guide for small scale social research projects* (p. 191). Buckingham: Open University Press: ISBN 0335198066. Available at: https://archive.org/details/goodresearchguid00dens_0/page/182/mode/2up/search/overload

Dey, I. (1993). *Qualitative data analysis: A user-friendly guide for social scientists* (pp. 85, 201). New York: Routledge: ISBN 9780203412497.

Forte, T. (2023). *The PARA method*. Profile Books Limited: ISBN: 978 10081 9542, 978 10081 9559.

Gill, J., & Johnson, P. (2002). *Research methods for managers* (3rd ed., p. 169). Sage: ISBN: 0857023489.

McCloud, S. (2023). *Qualitative versus quantitative research methods and data analysis, simply psychology*. https://www.simplypsychology.org/qualitative-quantitative.html

Polit, D.F., & Beck, C.T. (2013). *Essentials of nursing research: Appraising evidence for nursing practice* (8th ed.). Philadelphia, PA: Wolters Kluwer/Lippincott Williams & Wilkins: ISBN: 451176791, 978-1451176797

Stevenson University Library. (2023). *Research tips*. https://stevenson.libguides.com/

Trow, M. (1957). Comment on: Participant observation and interviewing: A Comparison. *Human Organization, 16* (4), 33–35. doi:10.17730/humo.16.3.cx277m417x00w647

A selection of useful resources

21st Century Doctorate. https://www.qaa.ac.uk/scotland/development-projects/learning-from-international-practice/21st-century-doctorate

Arrow. https://arrow.tudublin.ie/

Baidu Scholar. http://research.baidu.com/

BASE (Bielefeld Academic Search Engine). https://www.base-search.net/
CORE. https://core.ac.uk/
Discover PhDs. https://www.discoverphds.com/
Embassy of Good Science. https://embassy.science/wiki/Main_Page
Ethos. https://ethos.bl.uk/Home.do;jsessionid=48B2B2221BF22CD0CF
    65240BD97D95F6
Foster Open Science. https://www.fosteropenscience.eu/
KU Leuven. https://research.kuleuven.be/en/career/phd
Mendeley. https://www.mendeley.com/
Science.gov. https://www.science.gov/

6 Thesis structure, literature review, and checklists

INSIGHT

"Read dissertations from your sector."

Supervisor, Assistant Head of School
of Media, PhD, History

▶ INTRODUCTION

Organising your work to complete a literature review and structure a thesis is discussed in this chapter. The checklists aim to help you work out what is required to deliver a superb thesis, and access literature aimed at strengthening the thesis content towards the end of the programme.

The chapter closes with a summary of key concepts and recommended exercises and introduces the theme of *Part III: Progress*.

DOI: 10.4324/9781003413691-8

▶ LITERATURE REVIEW

A doctoral literature review takes time to produce and adapts throughout the doctoral journey. It presents to the reader the author's understanding of current research, key areas of examination, debate, and dialogue, and demonstrates the author's scholarship. It presents the current state of the art and sets the scene for the research topic, the methodology, and the rationale for the study. The literature review should stand on its own and be written with the understanding that it will be read by scholars and experts in the field. It needs to be bullet-proof, addressing the demands of experts who are passionate about the subject, willing to defend standards in their area and open to new insights. A well-researched literature review is a pleasure to read regardless of the complexity of the subject matter and an essential requirement for a thesis and publications. It acts as the foundation for the study, and when there are areas of weakness, the credibility of the work and the doctoral candidate are compromised.

It is important to define what counts as credible content within a literature review. It includes scholarly arguments and research studies discussed in books, journal articles, government reports, historical records, and academic websites. For instance, if an item on climate change research appears in mainstream media, it is prudent to go to the original source of the research, verify the key findings, and cite the original author rather than the media website. It is essential to clarify the language, structure, and format of conventional literature reviews in your discipline and research area. Furthermore, engaging with academic writing programmes, coaching, and guidance can help refine your skills.

Candidates are faced with competing perceptions of importance, value, and relevance between peers, disciplines and siloed ways of working. Researching the literature review often uncovers similar systems, processes, and conclusions across disciplines and research conducted in isolation from other areas of expertise. Sometimes, a supervisor will recommend a particular approach or suggest that literature from within rather than outside the area of specialisation is cited. Complying with and accepting scholarly conventions can be a challenge for non-academic candidates. Also, the practice of repeating and emphasising points within a document, which at first glance, offers no added value. Be open to feedback and consider the best next steps that allow you to progress AND showcase the key points and insights in the literature review.

Language and complexity: some academics argue that some level of difficulty and struggle is essential to understand an argument, concept, or proposal. They say that dense language comes with the territory. My view is that the purpose of the literature review is to share current thinking and include information that enables the user to critically analyse a specific research topic. Nevertheless, it is useful to examine whether complex language and the use of specific terms to demonstrate expertise and knowledge or presenting accurate, arguments and insights to promote understanding for the reader are required to progress.

A literature review examines the following

1. What has been written on the topic and key themes in the literature.
2. The key theories, hypotheses, concepts, and issues related to the topic.
3. Issues and gaps which the research topic can address or fill.
4. Key authors (established and emerging) whose insights are important to the research topic.

Points to consider when developing the literature review

1. Know your topic. Conduct the initial search to gain a general understanding of the topic and notice key patterns, insights, or potential gaps.
2. What is the purpose of the research and the purpose of the literature review?
3. Who is it for?
4. What does the reader need to know about the research and the topic?
5. What does the reader need to know about the research(er) or research team?

6. Update content/list of sources as more insights emerge and adapt the research question/hypothesis.
7. After supervisor and peer feedback, an annual review, a conference, and the viva reassess and identify material that is kept, adapted, or removed from the literature review.
8. Key question: Does the literature review present appropriate, accurate information on the topic and state of the art so readers can critically review and consider the content of the research, research question/hypothesis, findings, and recommendations?
9. If someone does not know the author (or research team), what do they need to know to get the most insight, value, and understanding of the research topic and acknowledge that the researcher is a credible contribution?
10. Are there any gaps or inconsistencies that need to be acknowledged or addressed in the review?
11. Are the references, citations, and sources of information correct?
12. What will it take to make this literature review relevant, impactful, and of genuine value to the reader and scholarly discourse?

INSIGHT

"It can feel like you are reading 100 articles for 100 hours, which end up as two sentences in your review."

Focusmate conversation

Literature review checklist and questions

It is good research practice to keep notes and records of information such as articles, journals, books, and presentations that have been accessed throughout the doctoral journey (Hart, 1998; see Tables 6.1, 6.2, and 6.3).

Things to consider towards the end of the literature review. Ask yourself.

TABLE 6.1 Start and middle stage. Taking notes for a literature review

STEP 1: When reviewing the literature and taking notes, ask:

1. What is the purpose of the paper?
2. What is the title of the paper, and who are the authors?
3. What approach was used to research the area?
4. List the findings and conclusions.
5. Briefly explain ways that this article/paper relates to other publications in the field.
6. In what way does it contribute to new knowledge and scholarly dialogue?
7. Are there any limitations, strengths, or weaknesses that need to be documented?
8. In what way does it link to your work?
9. List three key points that are of value in this paper.

STEP 2: Document and upload notes in your preferred system

Start and middle stage. Taking notes for a literature review. © 2023 Sinéad Hewson.

TABLE 6.2 Middle stage. literature review questions

1. What must I include in the literature review to demonstrate the depth and breadth of the sector and current state of the art?
2. Does the current version of the literature review go beyond recording the opinions and findings of others in the content? In what way specifically? Have I identified articles that challenge my research assumptions? In what way do they add value to the review?
3. Does the content and critique within the literature review suggest that there is potential for further research in this area? In what way (specifically)?
4. Does the content of the literature review clearly demonstrate my, the author's, understanding within and across theories?
5. Do I look as if I know what I am talking about? Are the cited sources of information relevant to the chapter/document?
6. Does the literature review contain the historical development of scholarship in the sector and how these developments feed into the current state of research (the art)?
7. Does the current version of the literature review demonstrate my expertise in the field and that I am an authority in this field of research?
8. Is there anything I am missing that could undermine the credibility of the work, my reputation, or the research?

Middle stage. Literature review questions. © 2023 Sinéad Hewson.

TABLE 6.3 Middle to end stage. literature review checklist

STEP 1: When reviewing the literature review, ask if I have:

1. Clearly presented the current state of the art.
2. Identified gaps, inconsistencies, or shortcomings in current knowledge.
3. Demonstrated that the doctoral study builds on existing work.
4. Demonstrated that I know the area very well.
5. Demonstrated that I am familiar with the most important topics, issues, and studies.
6. Identified areas for future research.
7. Indicated whether evidence is limited, contradictory, or inconclusive.
8. Identified and presented different theories, trends, and themes.
9. Present differing viewpoints.
10. Ensured that the content is relevant to my research.
11. Used primary sources in the literature review.
12. Cited credible and trustworthy sources such as peer-reviewed journals and online sources.
13. Presented material professionally and coherently following the practises and writing style of my area of expertise.
14. Adopted a consistent, relatable academic writing style.
15. Checked that references are up to date and correct.
16. Checked for errors and proofread the document (spelling, punctuation, grammar, language).
17. Explained and justified the proposed methodological approaches.
18. Clearly articulate how the work adds to the current debate.
19. Checked that it meets submission requirements (word count, citation format, etc.)

STEP 2: Circulate for supervisor feedback or peer review.

Middle to end stage. Literature review checklist. © 2023 Sinéad Hewson.

▶ GENERIC THESIS STRUCTURE AND CHECKLIST

This section follows the structure of a typical doctoral thesis and is used to help you work out the format of the final version of your work and how you present it for the final examination. A credible thesis contains clear, accurate information. It is easy to understand and academically written following the convention of your area of expertise. The structure is logical, coherent, and easy to follow. Ideally, every word, phrase, and paragraph should have a clear purpose. Citations and references are correct, with no typos or grammatical or factual errors. Keep this in mind as you progress through this chapter.

In addition, criteria and headings differ across subject areas, geographic locations, and institutions; therefore, it is important to customise the material. Proactively contact supervisors and university librarians and ask for sector-specific resources that are worth exploring and look at the selection of useful resources at the end of the chapter.

Carefully consider how to use the pointers in this chapter to aid progression, document the work accurately, contribute to new knowledge, and finish your doctorate. Adapt and build on the checklist content. Delete items that are not relevant to your area of study.

The first part of the generic thesis structure contains a typical table of contents (see Table 6.9), which acts as a checklist for each chapter in the dissertation. Start working on this in the early to middle stages of your doctoral programme and use it as a marker to help identify areas you may have overlooked or are uncertain about in your work.

Context

The generic thesis in this chapter follows the thesis format recommended by my supervisor. I developed the template, initially for personal use to get a better understanding of what was expected in a thesis. Although I read dissertations, examined the literature, and reviewed advice from academic writers, mentors, and experts, the level of detail, volume of information (Bloomberg, 2023; Bloomberg and Volpe, 2008; Kamler and Thomson, 2006), and variety of opinions available was too much. Information was presented through an academic lens, and I did not relate to it. I hope that the generic thesis structure will help mature and part-time users identify what they need to develop, and present in the thesis or commentary document they submit for the final defence.

During the thesis writing phase, incompletion rates tend to increase because candidates underestimate the time necessary to structure and format their work or experience a sense of over-whelm and stop. I hope that presenting the typical structure in manageable, bite-size pieces and will encourage you to integrate it into your work plan (Table 4.4. Exercise: Right from the start. Early-stage planning) will mitigate your dropout risk and the All But Dissertation (ABD) title. It is an unofficial title describing someone who has completed all of their doctoral coursework and has not submitted their thesis. US statistics indicate that up to 50% of doctoral candidates do not complete or submit their dissertations (Sowell et al., 2008; Young et al., 2019).

Format

This section is written in plain English and highlights key parts of the thesis.

The generic thesis structure aims to help you create an outline of what the dissertation could look like. It will adapt and develop throughout the programme (see Tables 6.4 through to 6.19). Set up a meeting with your supervisor or academic writing team to under-stand their expectations of what is essential to include in the thesis or (depending on your doctorate) commentary presentation. The interviews highlighted that mature students do not need to be spoon-fed, they need a steer in the right direction and clarity of expectations. That is the purpose of the following pages.

My advice is to block a half or even a full day to go through this. Work in a quiet area where you will not be disturbed. Review the material and develop your version. Look at the work plan created in Chapter 4, break the activity into smaller tasks and consider when, where, and how you will work on your thesis. Be realistic.

The sections of the typical thesis are presented as separate check-list tables. Some of the tables contain trigger or starter phrases, which writers and academics use to kick-start a piece of text. This tactic is known as syntactic borrowing and is useful to start the process of shaping the content and form of the thesis.

Front matter

TABLE 6.4 Thesis: Title page

Date:	Version:

Purpose:

1. Clearly and concisely describe the research topic or problem.
2. Outline the scope of the study.
3. Identify the author(s) as the owner(s) of the work.

Example:

[Insert University name/logo]

[Insert thesis title]

[Insert: sub-heading to explain the topic]

This doctoral thesis is submitted to [insert: University Name]

in candidature for admission to the [insert: PhD or doctoral] register

[insert: candidate's first name and surname]

[insert: date, month and year]

[insert: school or faculty name]

[insert: faculty or college name]

[insert: university name]

Supervisor(s):

[insert: supervisor(s) title, first name and second name]

IT SHOULD CONTAIN	ASK
Title page: (follow university guidelines) ○ Title. ○ Author's full name. ○ The degree to be conferred. ○ University, department, and college. ○ Month and year of approval. ○ Supervisor(s). ○ Student number. *Format: (follow university guidelines)* ○ Check title page margins ○ Check margins for the rest of the document ○ Check title page text and fonts ○ Check text and fonts for the rest of the document	1. Does the thesis title clearly convey what the thesis is about? 2. Does the thesis title convey the essence, purpose, and type of study? 3. Is it understandable? 4. Does it contain keywords to make the work findable in databases such as EThOS (British Library), ERIC (the Education Resources Information Center), Dissertation Abstracts International and OATAD (Open Access Theses and Dissertations)? 5. Is the language concise, accurate, relevant to my area of expertise and understandable?

(Continued)

TABLE 6.4 (Continued)

Date:	Version:

PRIORITY AREAS

1.
2.
3.

WHAT MAKES THIS SECTION EXCELLENT?

1.
2.
3.

Thesis: Title page. © 2023 Sinéad Hewson.

TABLE 6.5 Thesis: Declaration page

Date:	Version:

Purpose:

1. Signed confirmation that the thesis is the author's original work and complies with research integrity and ethical guidelines set by the awarding institution (Embassy of Good Science, 2022; ALLEA, 2023).

Example:

[sample] Declaration

I certify that this thesis which I now submit for examination for the award of [insert: PhD or doctorate], is entirely my own work and has not been taken from the work of others, save and to the extent that such work has been cited and acknowledged within the text of my work.

This thesis was prepared according to the regulations for graduate study by research of [insert university name] and has not been submitted in whole or in part for another award in any other third level institution.

The work reported on in this thesis conforms to the principles and requirements of [insert university name]'s guidelines for ethics in research.

[insert university name] has permission to keep, lend or copy this thesis in whole or in part, on condition that any such use of the material of the thesis be duly acknowledged.

Signature _____ Date _____

Candidate: [insert candidate name in full]

(Continued)

TABLE 6.5 (Continued)

Date:	Version:

IT SHOULD CONTAIN	ASK
Declaration page: (follow university guidelines)	1. Does the declaration confirm that the thesis is the author's original work and is presented as part of the requirements for a doctorate award?
o Title applied for.	
o University, department, and college.	
o Candidate's full name and signature.	
o Date.	
Format: (follow university guidelines)	2. Is it dated and signed?
o Check the declaration page margins.	3. Does it confirm that the study follows research integrity and ethical guidelines set by the awarding institution?
o Check margins for the rest of the document.	
o Check the declaration page text and fonts.	
o Check text and fonts for the rest of the document.	

PRIORITY AREAS

1.
2.
3.

WHAT MAKES THIS SECTION EXCELLENT?

1.
2.
3.

Thesis: Declaration page. © 2023 Sinéad Hewson.

TABLE 6.6 Thesis: Copyright page

Date:	Version:

Purpose:Clearly states who legally owns the created material and has the right to control its distribution and ownership.

Sample text:

© [insert: year] [insert: candidate name(s)] [insert: university name]
All Rights Reserved

(*Continued*)

TABLE 6.6 (Continued)

Date:	Version:

IT SHOULD CONTAIN	ASK

Copyright page: (follow university guidelines)

o Copyright symbol.
o Year.
o Author's full name.
o University name.
o All Rights Reserved/ Open Access/ Creative Commons text.
o Check that the page complies with the doctoral guidelines of the awarding body and their copyright requirements.

Format: (follow university guidelines)

o Check margins for the copyright page.
o Check margins for the rest of the document.
o Check the text and fonts for the copyright page.
o Check the text and fonts for the rest of the document.

Note:

1. Copyright is the legal right of the owner of the original material to control the copying and ownership of that material. For instance, the author of a research document can safeguard the work as soon as the work appears in a tangible form of expression. Copyright law covers various works, from paintings, photographs, and illustrations to musical compositions, sound recordings, computer programs, books, poems, blog posts, dissertations, architectural works, and plays.
2. Open Access/Open Science is a model which allows open access to scholarly research within certain legal limits. It aims to make research more findable, shareable and accessible. An Open Access thesis is available publicly when it is published.
3. Clarify the policy with your institution and agree the wording to be included re: copyright and open access.

DISCLAIMER:
The information on this Copyright page is an example and for illustration purposes. It does not constitute legal or professional advice on behalf of the author or publisher. Follow the copyright guidelines set by the awarding institution assessing the work. If necessary, seek legal advice to protect the work.

PRIORITY AREAS

1.
2.
3.

WHAT MAKES THIS SECTION EXCELLENT?

1.
2.
3.

Thesis: Copyright page. © 2023 Sinéad Hewson.

TABLE 6.7 Thesis: Abstract

Date:	Version:

Purpose:

1. A summary description of the study (the entire thesis).
2. Formatted for inclusion in dissertation and abstract platforms and international use.

IT SHOULD CONTAIN

Abstract Page: (follow university guidelines)

- o 350 words
- o Statement of the problem
- o Purpose
- o Scope
- o Research tradition/method
- o Data sources
- o Methodology
- o Key findings
- o Implications
- o Written from the perspective of an outside reader
- o Original text
- o Finalise when the thesis is complete
- o Keywords

Format: (follow university guidelines)

- o Check the margins for the abstract page.
- o Check margins for the rest of the document.
- o Check text and fonts for the abstract page.
- o Check text and fonts for the rest of the document.

ASK

1. Does the abstract accurately describe the study?
2. Is it concise and clearly written?
3. Is there a problem statement?
4. Does it explain the purpose and scope of the study?
5. Does it briefly mention the scope, the research approach (tradition), data sources, and methodology?
6. Does it summarise the key findings and implications of the study?
7. It is written from the perspective of an outside reader.
8. Does it meet the text limit and submission requirements of the awarding institution?
9. Is the text original?
10. Confirm that this text is the latest version of the abstract.
11. Is the language accurate and clear?
12. Does it use keywords to aid findability?

PRIORITY AREAS

1.
2.
3.

WHAT MAKES THIS SECTION EXCELLENT?

1.
2.
3.

Thesis: Abstract. © 2023 Sinéad Hewson.

TABLE 6.8 Thesis: Acknowledgement and dedication

Date: *Version:*

Purpose:

To acknowledge and thank contributors. A dedication is optional.

Example:

[sample] Dedication

I am eternally grateful to [insert name] for giving me space to work out my ideas and their advice to reign things in when I lost focus. They generously shared opinion and insight with words of encouragement to remain curious, question and keep going. [insert name] who directed structure, content, challenged and pushed me to finish. I was blessed to have two fantastic mentors and advisors. Thank you.

To my network of cousins, friends, colleagues, academics and strangers who helped along the way. They recommended people, gave feedback and insight on the direction of the research. [insert name] and the library team in [insert university name]. Thank you!

My family in [insert location] especially [insert names] who looked out for me on every visit. [insert name] who read the early material and gave honest feedback, [insert names] who supported me in the final weeks sorting out transcripts. Thank you!!

[insert names] my beautiful family in [insert location] – this is for you. Although our circumstances changed at beginning of the research journey. We weathered the storm and found a way through to pursue this dream together. Life is blossoming again, and I love you both.

[insert name and signature]

TABLE 6.8 (Continued)

Date:	Version:

IT SHOULD CONTAIN	ASK

Acknowledgements page: (follow university guidelines)

o Acknowledgement text.
o List of supervisors, peers, promoters, committee members, colleagues, industry, friends, and family members who supported the application process, the doctoral research, and the candidate.
o List of funders/research sponsors.

Dedication: (follow university guidelines)

o Dedication text (optional).

Format: (follow university guidelines)

o Check margins for the acknowledgement page.
o Check margins for the dedication page.
o Check margins for the rest of the document.
o Check text and fonts for the acknowledgement page.
o Check text and fonts for the dedication page.
o Check text and fonts for the rest of the document.

ASK

1. Have I included the right people?
2. Did anyone on the list request anonymity?
3. Is the content and tone appropriate?
4. Is the copy appropriate?
5. Are quotes/references properly credited?

PRIORITY AREAS

1.
2.
3.

WHAT MAKES THIS SECTION EXCELLENT?

1.
2.
3.

Thesis: Acknowledgment and dedication. © 2023 Sinéad Hewson.

TABLE 6.9 Thesis: Table of contents

Date:	Version:

Purpose:
1. Organise and present content in a logical order.
2. Provide a detailed overview of the thesis.
3. Acts as a signpost for readers to navigate the work.

[Sample] Table of contents

Title page	3
Declaration page	4
Copyright page	5
Abstract	6
Acknowledgements, dedication	7
Table of contents	8
List of tables, list of figures	9
List of terms	10
Chapter 1: Introduction	11
Chapter 2: literature review	13
Chapter 3: Methodology	16
Chapter 4: Findings	19
Chapter 5: Analysis and synthesis	21
Chapter 6: Conclusions	24
Back matter (appendices)	27

(*Continued*)

TABLE 6.9 (Continued)

Date:	*Version:*

IT SHOULD CONTAIN	CHECK THAT
Table of contents: (follow university guidelines) o Outline of the entire thesis. o Headings: named and checked against the page number. o Subheadings: named and checked against the page number. o Chapters: named and checked against the page number. o Major sections: named and checked against the page number. o Back Matter: named and checked against the page number. *Format: (follow university guidelines)* o Check margins for the contents page. o Check margins for the rest of the document. o Check text and fonts for the contents page. o Check text and fonts for the rest of the document.	1. Headings and subheadings accurately reflect the material contained in the main body of the thesis. 2. The layout and format comply with the awarding institution's guidelines. 3. The automated table of contents against the actual page numbers. 4. The headings and subheadings in the table of contents exactly match the headings and subheadings in the chapters. 5. The headings and subheadings are grammatically consistent (language, spelling, tone and tense).

PRIORITY AREAS

1.
2.
3.

WHAT MAKES THIS SECTION EXCELLENT?

1.
2.
3.

Thesis: Table of contents. © 2023 Sinéad Hewson.

TABLE 6.10 Thesis: List of tables

Date: Version:

Purpose:

1. Present a list of tabular information in the thesis.
2. Acts as a signpost to navigate the work.

IT SHOULD CONTAIN

List of tables: (follow university guidelines)

o A list of the tables used in the dissertation.
o Contains a table number and a description of the title.

Format: (follow university guidelines)

o Check margins for the list of tables page.
o Check margins for the rest of the document.
o Check text and fonts for the list of tables page.
o Check text and fonts for the rest of the document.

CHECK THAT

1. Tables are named and checked against page number.
2. The accuracy of an automatically generated list of tables against actual table and page numbers.
3. Table numbers and descriptions in the list of tables are worded exactly the same as those in the text.
4. Tabular headings and subheadings clearly and concisely reflect the content and are correctly placed within the chapters.
5. Layout and format according to university guidelines.
6. Check that the descriptors are consistent (language, grammar, spelling, and tone).

PRIORITY AREAS

1.
2.
3.

WHAT MAKES THIS SECTION EXCELLENT?

1.
2.
3.

Thesis: List of tables. © 2023 Sinéad Hewson.

TABLE 6.11 Thesis: List of figures/diagrams

Date:	Version:

Purpose:

1. Lists figures and diagrams used in the thesis.
2. Acts as a signpost to navigate the work.

IT SHOULD CONTAIN

list of figures/diagrams: (follow university guidelines)

o Figures and diagrams used in the dissertation.
o Figures: named and checked against page number.
o Diagrams: named and checked against page number.

Format: (follow university guidelines)

o Check margins for the list of figures/diagrams page.
o Check margins for the rest of the document.
o Check text and fonts for the list of figures/diagrams page.
o Check text and fonts for the rest of the document.

CHECK THAT

1. Figures/diagrams are named and checked against page number.
2. The accuracy of an automatically generated list of figures/diagrams against actual table and page numbers.
3. Figure/diagram numbers and descriptions in the list are worded exactly the same as those in the text.
4. The descriptors are clear and concisely reflect the content and are correctly placed within the chapters.
5. Layout and format according to university guidelines.
6. Check that the descriptors are consistent (language, grammar, spelling and tone).

PRIORITY AREAS

1.
2.
3.

WHAT MAKES THIS SECTION EXCELLENT?

1.
2.
3.

Thesis: List of figures/diagrams. © 2023 Sinéad Hewson.

TABLE 6.12 Thesis: List of terms

Date:	*Version:*

Purpose:

1. Outline the terms and acronyms used in the thesis.
2. Acts as a reference point to navigate the work and aid the user.

IT SHOULD CONTAIN

list of terms: (follow university guidelines)

o List the terms and acronyms used in the dissertation and their meaning.

Format: (follow university guidelines)

o Check margins for the list of terms page.
o Check margins for the rest of the document.
o Check text and fonts for the list of terms page.
o Check text and fonts for the rest of the document.

CHECK THAT

1. The terms are accurate, and acronyms are correct.
2. The terms and acronyms are cited consistently in the list of terms and throughout the thesis.
3. The layout and format comply with university guidelines.

PRIORITY AREAS

1.
2.
3.

WHAT MAKES IT EXCELLENT?

1.
2.
3.

Thesis: List of terms. © 2023 Sinéad Hewson.

Chapter 1: Introduction

TABLE 6.13 Thesis: Introduction

Date: *Version:*

Purpose:

1. Orientates readers on the purpose and content of the thesis.
2. Introduces the thesis and the research problem.
3. Set the scene for the study (the importance of the topic, the gap in knowledge, the purpose and value of the study).
4. Reads as a concise, stand-alone document.
5. It is understandable, informative, and precise.

Trigger/starter phrases (Morley, 2003):

o The issue of … has recently grown in importance.
o This investigation explores the …
o It considers whether the position of ….
o To date, there has been little agreement on …
o This study moves the discussion forward on …
o This study builds on … and contributes …

IT SHOULD CONTAIN	CHECK THAT
Chapter 1:Introduction and context review o Introduction. o Problem statement. o Statement of purpose. o Research question/hypothesis. o Methodology overview. o Rationale, significance, and contribution to new knowledge. o Role of researcher. o Research and researcher assumptions. o Definition of key terminology. o Chapter-by-chapter organisation of the thesis. o Chapter summary. *References and quotes: (follow university guidelines)* o Check accuracy and logic with content. o Check and verify source and DOI. o Follow the recommended citation format.	1. It contains a brief outline of the thesis, context review, and the motivation for the research. 2. Key terms are clearly defined and their role in the research. 3. It sets the scene for the study. 4. Language is informative, concise, and accurate. 5. The thesis structure contains an overview of what will be found in the remainder of the document.

(Continued)

TABLE 6.13 (Continued)

Date: *Version:*

Format: (follow university guidelines)

- o Check margins for the rest of the document.
- o Check text and fonts for the rest of the document.
- o Check the format and headings against the table of contents.
- o Proofread the chapter.

PRIORITY AREAS

1.
2.
3.

WHAT MAKES THIS SECTION EXCELLENT?

1.
2.
3.

Thesis: Introduction. © 2023 Sinéad Hewson.

Chapter 2: Literature review

TABLE 6.14 Thesis: Literature review

Date: *Version:*

Purpose:

1. Provide an overview of current scholarly knowledge (theories, models, and concepts).
2. Identify where the study sits within the academic/sectoral landscape.
3. Identify gaps or problems with the current knowledge and ways a study can address that gap.
4. Provide a theoretical or conceptual framework of the study to guide the research, analysis, and synthesis of the findings later in the process.

(*Continued*)

TABLE 6.14 (Continued)

Date:	Version:

Trigger/starter phrases:

o Includes a literature review as an analysis of ...
o ... and ... are also explored.
o Concepts including ... are discussed.
o The chapter proposes definitions of ...
o Advances specifically relating to ... are ...
o Although the chapter provides a ... perspective of the study, the content is relevant throughout the thesis.
o The literature review specifically shaped the methodology and lays the foundation for the conclusions in the closing chapter.
o The Context Review presented later in the chapter sets the scene for the study.

IT SHOULD CONTAIN

Chapter 2:
Literature review

Introduction:

o Details the content and scope of the literature review.
o Explains the organisation of the chapter.
o Provides information on how the literature review was conducted.

Review of literature:

o Is relevant and relates to the problem statement, the purpose of the study, and the research question/hypothesis.
o Clearly indicates what will be covered and why.
o Synthesises, compares, and contrasts different bodies of work.
o Identifies gaps, issues, and differences of opinion in the literature.
o Justifies the proposed research approach.

Conceptual framework:

o It provides a structure and basic understanding of the factors at play in the doctoral study.
o Contains concepts, variables, and connections drawn from the literature review to guide the research, methodology, and analysis of the findings.

CHECK THAT

1. Content is relevant and relates to the problem statement, the purpose of the study, and the research question/hypothesis.
2. It cites primary and secondary sources of information from scholarly journals and publications.
3. It is coherent and well-organised, initially focusing on broad themes and then on a specific area.
4. That the conceptual framework is logical, easy to follow, and credible.
5. Includes a diagram mapping the key factors to aid understanding.
6. Is factual, accurate, and concise.

(*Continued*)

TABLE 6.14 (Continued)

Date: *Version:*

Summary

○ Synthesises key points from the literature
   review.

References and quotes

○ Check accuracy and logic with content.
○ Check and verify source and DOI.
○ Follow the recommended citation format.

Format

○ Check margins for the rest of the document.
○ Check text and fonts for the rest of the
   document.
○ Check format and headings against the
   table of contents.
○ Proofread the chapter

PRIORITY AREAS

1.
2.
3.

WHAT MAKES THIS SECTION EXCELLENT?

1.
2.
3.

Thesis: Literature review. © 2023 Sinéad Hewson.

Chapter 3: Methodology

TABLE 6.15 Thesis: Methodology

Date:	Version:

Purpose:

1. It describes the methodology (the approach) used to address the research question/hypothesis.
2. It justifies the rationale and reasoning for that approach.
3. It describes the research context, sample, and inclusion criteria.
4. Clearly describes data collection and analysis methods.
5. Details the study design, procedures, and policies.
6. Demonstrates knowledge of research theory of the PhD candidate/author(s).

Trigger/starter phrases:

o The chapter gives an in-depth account of the methodology used to ...
o The methodology is documented, and the process of ... is outlined ...
o This methodology has a number of advantages, such as ...
o Limitations to the study design include ...
o Data were gathered from ...
o Once the research topic was identified, a research plan was developed to ...

IT SHOULD CONTAIN

Chapter 3: Methodology

Introduction:

o Restate the research problem and purpose of the study.
o Explain the organisation of the chapter.

Research approach and rationale:

o Explain the research approach used.
o Gives reasons to justify that choice to address the research question.

Research context:

o Describes and justifies the selection of the research setting-based choices, including the research philosophy, research type, research strategy timing, and resources.

CHECK THAT

1. The material in this chapter is trustworthy and validated with relevant, correctly cited scholarly literature.
2. Content is coherent and well-organised.
3. The methodology is clearly explained and properly justified.
4. That the approach makes the study replicable (FAIR principles).
5. Uses where possible diagrams, figures and tables to illustrate an important point.

(Continued)

TABLE 6.15 (Continued)

Date:	Version:

Sampling criteria and data sources

- o Explain and justify the research design and selection criteria.
- o Describe the sample size, characteristics, demographics, and ethical considerations relating to the study.

Data collection methods

- o Description of data collection methods, resources, policies, procedures, timings, and responsibilities for data collection.

Data analysis methods

- o Details of the methods and tools used to analyse data (manual, computer, AI).

Strengths and limitations

- o Discuss the strengths, weaknesses, limitations, and transferability of the study.

References and quotes

- o Check accuracy and logic with content.
- o Check and verify source and DOI.
- o Follow the recommended citation format.

Format

- o Check margins for the rest of the document.
- o Check text and fonts for the rest of the document.
- o Check the format and headings against the table of contents.
- o Proofread the chapter.

PRIORITY AREAS

1.
2.
3.

WHAT MAKES THIS SECTION EXCELLENT?

1.
2.
3.

Thesis: Methodology. © 2023 Sinéad Hewson.

Chapter 4: Findings

TABLE 6.16 Thesis: Findings

Date: *Version:*

Purpose:

1. Organise and objectively report the study's main findings in detail.
2. It acts as the foundation for the analysis, conclusions, and recommendations chapters of the thesis.

Trigger/starter phrases:

- A positive correlation was found between ... and ...
- The results, as seen in ... indicate that ...
- No significant reduction in ... was found.
- This chapter provides a detailed analysis of ...
- Throughout the sections, the data gained from ... will be analysed and utilised.
- The data gathered using the methods described in Chapter ... will be critically evaluated based on the theories, frameworks, and contexts outlined in Chapter [insert name].
- This body of empirical evidence will (hopefully) underpin the analysis and synthesis chapter and the conclusions and proposals of the study.
- ... will be used to illustrate key points and different communication perspectives.

IT SHOULD CONTAIN	CHECK THAT
Chapter 4: *Findings:* *Introduction:* o Provides a summary and rationale for the data analysis. o Describes the organisation of the chapter according to research question/hypothesis and conceptual framework. *Findings:* o Links findings to the problem, research question/hypothesis, and design. o Uses information directly from the research and synthesises findings through text, tables, diagrams, and graphics. o Headings guide the reader through the findings according to the research question/hypothesis, themes, or organisational schemes. o Inconsistent or unexpected data and reasons for the differences are cited.:::	1. The material contains enough detail to tell the story of the research findings. 2. The introduction reminds the reader of the purpose of the study. 3. The content is coherent and well-organised. 4. Uses where possible diagrams, figures and tables to illustrate an important point. 5. Findings are clear, trustworthy, transparent and objective. 6. Findings are presented following the format of the research question or hypothesis and/or themes identified through primary and secondary research. 7. Unexpected results are addressed appropriately. 8. The summary is clear for readers giving them an indication of what is to come in the final chapters.

(Continued)

TABLE 6.16 (Continued)

Date:	Version:

Summary

o Summarises key findings, insights, and explanations.
o Sets the tone and direction for the final thesis chapters.

References and quotes

o Check accuracy and logic with content.
o Check and verify source and DOI.
o Follow recommended citation format.

Format

o Check margins for the rest of the document.
o Check text and fonts for the rest of the document.
o Check the format and headings against the table of contents.
o Proofread the chapter.

PRIORITY AREAS

1.
2.
3.

WHAT MAKES THIS SECTION EXCELLENT?

1.
2.
3.

Thesis: Findings. © 2023 Sinéad Hewson.

Chapter 5:Analysis and synthesis

TABLE 6.17 Thesis:Analysis and synthesis

Date:	Version:

Purpose:

1. Identify patterns, themes, and insights that emerge from the findings.
2. Compare and contrast the findings across themes, context framework, and against existing work.
3. Discuss the meaning and implications of the findings.
4. Demonstrate a deep understanding of the work and its potential to contribute to new knowledge.
5. Positions the doctoral study as unique and original work.

Trigger/starter phrases:

o The analysis of the data uses the research methods and theoretical framework outlined earlier in the thesis and …
o The implications of the findings will be discussed in this chapter and can be summarised as follows …
o The underlying trends which emerged …
o There are similarities in … between the present study and those described by …
o It is possible to hypothesise that …
o An important issue emerging from these findings is …

IT SHOULD CONTAIN	CHECK THAT
Chapter 5 Analysis and synthesis Introduction o Describe the organisation of the chapter according to the research question/ hypothesis, themes, data collection methods, or conceptual framework.	1. The analysis is accurate and reflects the insights drawn from the research findings. 2. The content is credible, coherent, and well-organised. 3. The arguments are well thought through, trustworthy, transparent, and objective. 4. The analysis follows the format of the research question or hypothesis and/ or themes identified through primary and secondary research. 5. That the analysis links (and correspond) with points raised in earlier chapters.

(Continued)

TABLE 6.17 (Continued)

Date: *Version:*

Discussion:

o Tell the story of the research by describing, analysing, and synthesising the findings.
o Compare and contrast the results with work cited in the literature review. Comment on whether results are similar, different, unexpected, or build on existing knowledge.
o Compare and contrast results with the published work of others. Comment on whether results are similar, different, unexpected, or build on existing knowledge.
o Analyses and discusses the implications of expected and unexpected findings.
o Discuss the implications of the results, mentioning the strengths, weaknesses, limitations, and transferability of the study.
o Explain in what way the research question/hypothesis has been addressed.

6. That any charts, tables, or illustrations are accurate and located in the main body of the thesis or as an appendix.
7. The summary is clear for readers giving them an indication of what is to come in the closing chapter.
8. Ask: Have I answered the research question?
9. Ask: Does the chapter reflect the quality of the work? Is it credible?
10. Ask: Does the chapter structure follow the reporting guidelines of my discipline?
11. Ask: Does it help readers gain an understanding of what the data really means?
12. Reflect: In what ways does this analysis position me as an expert?

Summary:

o Summarises points from the analysis of the work.
o Signposts the focus and format of the closing chapter.

References and quotes:

o Check accuracy and logic with content.
o Check and verify source and DOI.
o Follow the recommended citation format.

Format:

o Check margins for the rest of the document.
o Check text and fonts for the rest of the document.
o Check the format and headings against the table of contents.
o Proofread the chapter.

(*Continued*)

TABLE 6.17 (Continued)

Date:	Version:

PRIORITY AREAS

1.
2.
3.

WHAT MAKES THIS SECTION EXCELLENT?

1.
2.
3.

Thesis: Analysis and synthesis. © 2023 Sinéad Hewson.

Chapter 6: Conclusion

TABLE 6.18 Thesis: Conclusion

Date:	Version:

Purpose:

1. Demonstrate the significance of the study.
2. Summarise the research findings and what they mean (concluding statements).
3. Discuss the implications of the findings and link back to issues raised in earlier chapters and the literature.
4. Consider the significance of the study in the sector and within the wider academic community.
5. Discuss the limitations of the study and recommendations for further examination and/or continuity of the research.

Trigger/starter phrases:

o   This study adds to the body of knowledge around …
o   This research confirms previous findings and contributes to our understanding of …
o   Although the study did not show …, it did substantiate …
o   The findings suggest there is merit in exploring …
o   This trend requires further analysis and would benefit from …
o   In light of this, recommendations for … and … include …
o   One point of note is …

(Continued)

TABLE 6.18 (Continued)

Date:	Version:

IT SHOULD CONTAIN	CHECK THAT
Chapter 6: Conclusion and Recommendations *Introduction:* o Describe the organisation of the chapter following the research question/hypothesis, themes, data collection methods, or conceptual framework. o Restates the research question/ hypothesis and purpose of the study. *Conclusions:* o Summarises new knowledge, insights, and learnings that emerged from the research. o Contains concluding statements and clear calls to action from the analysis of the findings. *Recommendations:* o Clear call to action. o Discusses topics that require further examination. o Recommendations for new research. o Contains a clear to action in academia and beyond (academia, sector, policy, wider community). *Summary:* o Summarise the chapter content and conclusions. o Highlight your contribution to academic discourse and new knowledge.	1. It sums up the research findings and includes a set of recommendations and next steps for the sector. 2. It refers to and build on points raised in earlier chapters. 3. The conclusions are accurate and reflect the insights drawn from the research findings and analysis. 4. The content is credible, coherent, and well-organised. 5. The arguments are well thought through, trustworthy, transparent, and objective. 6. The summary is clear for readers giving them an indication of what is to come in now that the doctoral study is complete. 7. There are no ambiguous or loose ends in the work. 8. Ask: Have I answered the research question? 9. Ask: Does the chapter reflect the quality of the work? Is it credible? 10. Ask: Does the chapter structure follow the reporting guidelines of my discipline? 11. Ask: Does the thesis structure follow the reporting guidelines of my discipline? 12. Ask: Does it help readers gain an understanding of the new knowledge which emerged from the study? 13. Reflect: In what ways does the entire body of work position me as an expert?

(*Continued*)

TABLE 6.18 (Continued)

Date:	Version:

Epilogue, Afterword, or Final Thoughts

o Personal reflection on the process and on insights that emerged during the study.
o Comment on the doctoral experience, personal/professional development, and growth.
o Lessons learned and insights from the research experience.

References and quotes
o Check accuracy and logic with content.
o Check and verify source and DOI.
o Follow the recommended citation format.

Format

o Check margins for the rest of the document.
o Check text and fonts for the rest of the document.
o Check the format and headings against the table of contents.
o Proofread the chapter.

PRIORITY AREAS

1.
2.
3.

WHAT MAKES THIS SECTION EXCELLENT?

1.
2.
3.

Thesis: Conclusion. © 2023 Sinéad Hewson.

Back matter

TABLE 6.19 Thesis: Back matter

Date:	Version:

Purpose:

1. Provides a list of references of books, resources, and academic work cited in the study.
2. Provides appendices containing additional material used in the research that the reader can refer to as needed.
3. Adds to the credibility and transparency of the research.
4. The references section attributes work fairly to peers.

Example (from author's thesis)

Appendix structure

    I. Interview format
   II. Briefing permission form
  III. Ethics permission form
  IV. Transcript approval form
   V. Privacy statement, security and use of data
  VI. Participant summary
 VII. Participant ID, profiles, permissions, company (and individual) ID
VIII. Transcripts and audio links
  IX. Researcher: self-reflection notes
   X. References and bibliography
   X. Glossary of terms

IT SHOULD CONTAIN	CHECK THAT
Back matter	1. The content is credible, coherent, and well-organised.
Appendices:	
References:	2. That the information is contained in the right part of the thesis.
o Comment on the doctoral experience, personal/professional development and growth.	3. References are properly cited and in alphabetical order.
o Lessons learnt and insights from the research experience.	4. There are no ambiguous or loose ends in the text.
Format:	5. Ask: Does the information reflect the quality of the work?
o Check margins for the rest of the document.	6. Ask: Does the back matter structure follow the reporting guidelines of my discipline/institution?
o Check text and fonts for the rest of the document.	
o Check the format and headings against the table of contents.	
o Check the page number or letter against the table of contents.	7. Ask: Does it help readers understand more about my research?
o Proofread the text.	

(*Continued*)

TABLE 6.19 (Continued)

Date:	Version:

PRIORITY AREAS

1.
2.
3.

WHAT MAKES THIS SECTION EXCELLENT?

1.
2.
3.

Thesis: Back matter. © 2023 Sinéad Hewson.

Reporting guidelines/university guidelines

Taking time to understand the thesis and reporting requirements can make the process of scoping the structure of the thesis easier (Thomas, 2016). In addition, candidates in the medical health area can access resources such as the EQUATOR Network which has access to over 500 reporting guidelines in specialised areas aimed at enhancing the quality and transparency of health research. Institutions such as the School of Engineering at Carnegie Mellon University and the University of Fine Arts, Helsinki provide thesis and dissertation standards on their websites which are useful to read.

Exercise: Connect back to the why

Reflect on the insights gained in through the literature review and developing the thesis. Is this part of the doctoral programme motivating you? Does it fulfil the "why am I doing this?" driver identified Part I: Motivation? What changes (if any) will you propose to align the project with your values? What needs to change, you or the focus of the literature review and thesis? In what ways can I demonstrate excellence throughout this process?

Exercise: Integrate into the work plan

Review the requirements for the literature review and for the thesis itself and break down the work into smaller tasks using the Generic thesis structure as a guide. Allocate blocks of time to complete the tasks, bit by bit. Integrate this into your workplan (Bloomberg, 2023; Bloomberg & Volpe, 2008).

Reflect: have I taken a SMART (specific, measurable, realistic and timely) approach to the work? Commit and allocate (undisturbed) time in your agenda to complete the work. Keep it simple and include breaks and time to reflect on the research and write.

▶ SUMMARY

The takeaways from this chapter are to treat the literature review and the drafting of the thesis as work plans within the bigger doctoral project. It is hoped that the generic chapter structure can be used as templates to customise formats for readers so that information is not lost during the writing process. To succeed, chunk the work into manageable tasks and dedicate blocks of time where you will be not disturbed to get the work done, to reflect, and think deeply.

Topics covered in this chapter are:

All But Dissertation
Literature review
Thesis structure
Own the process

▶ PART II: ORGANISATION SUMMARY

The takeaways from the chapters on organisation are to treat the doctoral process as a project with a start, a middle, and an end.

Organisation is key, and it is your responsibility to understand the policies and regulations of your institution and be clear on what is expected of you and others. Set up a dedicated workspace, and ensure you have access to equipment and resources to complete on time. Divide the work into manageable tasks and dedicate blocks of time where you will be not disturbed to get the work done, to reflect and think deeply.

▶ USEFUL RESOURCES AND REFERENCES

References

Bloomberg, L.D. (2023) *Completing your qualitative dissertation: A road map from beginning to end.* London: SAGE Publications. Kindle Edition: ISBN: 978-1-0718-6981-9.

Bloomberg, L. D., & Volpe, M. (2008). *Completing your qualitative dissertation: A roadmap from beginning to end. Part 1: Taking charge of yourself and your work.* Sage Publications. https://doi.org/10.4135/9781452226613

Embassy of Good Science. (2022). https://embassy.science/wiki-wiki/index.php/wiki-wiki/images/f/ff/The-Embassy-of-Good-Science-Declaration.pdf

Hart, C. (1998). *Doing a literature review: Releasing the social science imagination* (pp. 14–25). Houndmills: Palgrave Macmillan: ISBN: 0761959750, 9780761959755.

Kamler, B., & Thomson, P. (2006). *Helping doctoral students write: Pedagogies for supervision.* Oxon, UK: Routledge: ISBN: 0415346835, 0415346843, 0203969812.

Morley, J. (2023). *Academic phrasebank: An academic writing resource for students and researchers* (p. 7). Manchester: The University of Manchester. Kindle Edition: ASIN B08KWFR6MN.

Sowell, R., Zhang T., Redd, K., & Kin M.F., (2008) *PH.D. Completion and attrition: Analysis of baseline demographic data from the Ph.D. Completion project.* Washington, DC: Council of Graduate Schools. ISBN: 1-933042-18-4.81.

Thomas, D. (2016). *The PhD writing handbook* (p. 175). London: Palgrave Macmillan: ISBN: 978-1-137-49769-7.

Young, S. N., Vanwye, W. R., Schafer, M. A., Robertson, T. A., & Poore, A. V. (2019). Factors Affecting PhD Student Success. *International Journal of Exercise Science, 12* (1), 34–45 PMID: 30761191; PMCID: PMC6355122.

Resources

College of Engineering at Carnegie Mellon University. https://engineering.
cmu.edu/education/academic-policies/graduate-policies/thesis-
dissertation.html

Discover PhDs. www.discoverphds.com

EQUATOR NETWORK. https://www.equator-network.org/

ERIC. https://eric.ed.gov/

EThOS. https://bl.iro.bl.uk/

Franklin University. https://www.franklin.edu/degrees/doctoral

KU Leuven. https://research.kuleuven.be/en/career/phd

OATD. https://oatd.org/

RMIT University Library. https://emedia.rmit.edu.au/learninglab/sites/
default/files/Research_Starter_phrases_2014_Accessible.pdf

TU Delft PhD Guidelines. https://filelist.tudelft.nl/3mE/Onderzoek/
Graduate%20School/PhD-Guidebook_web.pdf

TU Dublin research graduate Handbook. https://www.tudublin.ie/
media/website/research/postgraduate-research/graduate-research-
school/documents/Graduate-Research-Regulations-1st-Edition.pdf

University of Fine Arts, Helsinki. https://student.uniarts.fi/general-info/
doctoral-thesis-project-in-fine-arts-examination-guidelines/

Part III
Progress

7

Progress, mindsets, and momentum

INSIGHTS

"Finish, it's worth the effort."

PhD, Social Sciences

▶ INTRODUCTION

Finishing is the focus of this and the following chapters, which explore *progress*, the third doctoral completion trigger. Finding ways to immerse yourself in the process, and recognising research breakthroughs and setbacks while balancing responsibilities outside of academia and day-to-day life is discussed. Progress and perfectionism are discussed, as well as recognising the triggers of when you hold yourself back. The following chapters are brief and designed for busy people.

Finished is better than perfect

Authors and researchers run into problems getting things done when they don't have an appropriate work process in place or find

DOI: 10.4324/9781003413691-10

themselves managing multiple roles, responsibilities, and time-consuming tasks outside of academia (Pitchforth et al., 2012). Some find themselves staring blankly at a computer screen at the end of a day bursting with work to-dos, parenting, caring, exercise, and day-to-day life. On paper, the time between eight and eleven at night looks like the perfect moment to read that article, submit a draft paper, or analyse data. Yet, there is not enough energy in the tank to concentrate. Suddenly, a purring cat video appears on social media, an hour has passed, and now there is no time to do something decent.

Turning up is the start of the process, taking action by switching into focus mode allows you to complete a task. Accessing the trigger that jolts you into action is embedded within the exercises that follow. Maintaining momentum, tracking progress, perfection, and patience all aim to increase awareness of how you get things done. This creates an opportunity for you to engage with the inner voice who wants you to stop, engage with it, and make resourceful choices.

Finished is better than perfect – easy to say, hard to do. This and the following chapters hope to address this.

▶ PROGRESS AND PERFECTION

> "It is difficult when you intuitively know all of the answers in your professional role and find yourself in a situation where believe you produced excellent work, yet, from an academic perspective, it is weak. When this happened, I questioned my ability and almost stopped."
>
> Part-time research doctorate

Progress is the forward or onward movement towards a destination. In doctoral PLGs, it relates to the completion of a significant project, task, or undertaking to progress to the next stage of a programme. An annual review is a formal recognition of progression to the next stage of a programme. The result is given as a recommendation for a candidate to advance, adapt, or abandon their doctorate.

Doctoral candidates hold themselves to high standards, expressing perfection as something that is right, wrong, or not good enough. They talk about the discomfort of being wrong, not meeting the standard they set for themselves or the burden of representation. "There is no time to fail at all, and I really feel like failing is a huge part of everything that you do" (International STEM student, Mantai 2019).

Logically, they understand that unexpected results and failure are pathways towards deeper learning, transformational growth, and innovation. The discomfort can trigger self-doubt so that energy shifts towards correctness and double-checking that they are right before taking action. It is important for mature students to recognise that is okay to be good enough for now and that being an expert in your sector does not make you a PhD (yet). Some academic institutions encourage candidates to adopt a completion mindset, by examining concepts, ideas, and actions that are focused on outputs that enable progress and completion and not necessarily aligned with the relevance or impact of new knowledge.

A fundamental part of the doctoral experience is to think critically and remain curious. Choosing to express perfection as something that has attained its purpose and is complete, as Aristotle proposed (Gonzalez, 1991), helps the creation of an inner sense of knowingness, possibility, pragmatism, and progression to the next stage.

Informal conversations with candidates using platforms such as Focusmate and LinkedIn highlight common themes such as the pressure of being right all the time, hesitancy and a sense of I should know better, when dealing with an unfamiliar academic environment, being unsure about something, expected behaviour, data, or how you speak up (Mantai, 2019). There is a drive amongst research integrity networks for the new generation of academics to be team-orientated, enable constructive dialogue with peers, and create formal and informal communities across different faculties so that they understand what's happening, share best practices (Lerouge & Hoi, 2020), and know that when they face challenges they are not alone. This is critical for part-time candidates who want their work to be perfect and are hesitant to ask for help in case it makes them appear incompetent.

▶ MINDSET AND COMPLETION

INSIGHT

"It was not difficult."
Part-time PhD by prior publication

"I felt I had something genuine to say, so I kept going."
Part-time PhD, Communication

"Turn up. Do the work. Track results."
Part-time PhD, History

A Growth Mindset is the belief that people can develop their abilities; it is fostered through hard work, strategies, focus, and perseverance. There is a requirement on many institutional programmes to adopt a Growth Mindset to enable curiosity, deep thinking, and critical analysis and contribute to scholarly discourse (Byron, 2009). A Fixed Mindset also has a place at the table because, says Dweck, "there are no great achievements without setbacks". The question for doctoral candidates is how to "persuade our fixed mindset persona to get on board with goals that spring from our growth mindset".

Exercise: Self-reflection. Doctoral Enablers

Examine the doctoral enablers in Table 7.1 and write down ways that you can address each one throughout the programme. Identify proactive steps you can take to take to address each enabler appropriately. Repeat this self-reflection exercise every 6–12

TABLE 7.1 Doctoral enablers

Completion Trigger	Enabler
Motivation	Understanding the motivation to undertake a doctorate. Affinity with the research topic. Candidate readiness. Understanding of expectations and goals.
Organisation	Understanding of expectations. Organisation and systems. Access to resources and tools. SMART goals. Supportive academic, personal, and physical environment. Financial support/plan.
Process	Understanding of the current status of the project. Reliable systems and processes. Tracking tasks, results, milestones, and progress. Time and budget management. Resources, tools, and access.
Wellbeing	Supportive academic and personal environment. Ownership of the doctoral process. Proactive management of health and wellbeing.

Doctoral enablers. © 2023 Sinéad Hewson.

months to examine whether you are on track with the programme and adjust as necessary.

Exercise: Embrace your Fixed Mindset

This exercise acknowledges that Fixed and Growth Mindsets co-exist. When you understand the characteristics of your Fixed Mindset, it is possible to remain in a Growth Mindset state even when triggered. This exercise helps you identify those triggers, to educate and understand more about your growth and Fixed Mindset (see Table 7.2). Dweck says that "great contributions are born out of curiosity and deep understanding". As your doctoral journey unfolds, both states of mind can and will contribute towards the work and significantly impact the personal transformation during the programme. Notice how your inner monologue changes, influencing what you think, how you act, what you feel,

TABLE 7.2 Embrace your Fixed Mindset

Step 1:
Be aware of triggers

1. Identify a recent time that triggered a Fixed Mindset.
2. What happened to summon this persona?
3. What did it whisper in your ear?
4. How did it make you feel?

Step 2:
Observe it, don't judge it

1. Give it a name.
2. Is it a name you associate with a situation?
3. Is it a name you don't like or want to associate with?
4. Does it remind you that you are somewhere you don't want to be?

Step 3:
Identify triggers

1. What triggers your Fixed Mindset?
2. Is it disagreements, failures, or disruptions? Is it being on the back foot, multiple responsibilities? Is it a deadline?
3. Who is this persona?
4. What does it make me think, feel, and do?
5. How does it affect those around me?

Step 4:
Converse with your Fixed Mindset persona

1. Have a dialogue with this persona and identify constructive ways it can help you reach your goal.
2. Write a letter to this persona and discuss ways to co-operate and bring out the best in you.
3. Next time it shows up. Have a discussion with it and respond to its concerns with something like, I don't have a solution to that problem YET. This is what I can do for now.

Note: Stretch, move, and take deep breaths as you go through this exercise. If issues unrelated to the doctorate emerge, reach out to your trusted advisor, mentor, or supervisor for support.

This exercise is an adaption of the Fixed Mindset Persona exercise by Professor Carol S. Dweck. Adapted.

Embrace your Fixed Mindset. Adapted with permission by Professor Carol S. Dweck.

and the decisions you make. Remember that you are shifting from mastery in one area of your life and a novice navigating the doctoral path. Be kind and learn from mistakes, misaligned expectations, and differences of opinion.

"I think one of the challenges, which is more personal, is That is a lonely journey, if you're not self-motivated, you can easily give up."

PhD, Theology

INSIDER TIPS

Set the tone for the day. Ask. What are the opportunities for learning and growth today? For me and the people around me? What is the best use of my time?

Responding to your Fixed Mindset persona. I don't have the solution just yet. This is what I can do for now.

Avoid spiralling downwards. Seek support if needed:

"Jumble the letters THESIS. Remove an S. That's how I feel." Doctoral Candidate, Spanish and Film [adapted]

Maintaining momentum

You made a long-term commitment to participate in a doctoral programme. In the short term, stress and frustration are tolerable when you know you are moving towards your goal. However, a significant part of the doctoral experience is working with the unknown. It takes time to process information and formulate ideas. If you are outside academia, allowing a concept to simmer, brew, and ferment can create a feeling of doing nothing, being on the road to nowhere. Although motivation can falter when you are in a Growth Mindset or high-performing state, the task you are working on is less likely to be disrupted, and you become more resilient to distractions.

Wavering momentum is normal, especially when tasked with completing a major task over a long period of time. Ongoing questioning, examining, reviewing, and uncertainty can slow or halt progress. Writers often say the act of turning up is enough, while elite athletes who might not feel like running, turn up, put on their trainers, and take the first step. Sometimes, turning up to do the work is enough.

Most PhDs are delivered late. Accept that it is likely to happen to you and set your own completion deadline. Delay does not mean failure, it's part of the doctoral process, as is your ability to proactively manage it (Tizazu Fetene & Tamrat, 2021; van de Schoot et al., 2013). Do so by adopting a completion mindset. This means having a clear sense of purpose, focusing on strengths and skills, being results-orientated, and being self-aware: patiently knowing when to push, when to stop, and when to pivot and change direction.

INSIDER TIPS

Plan early, and plan often. Complete small chunks of work piece by piece. Stick with it and celebrate. One set of bullet points, correcting a reference, and thinking about thinking are all progress.

Discernment. Choose your conferences carefully. Learn to say NO to tasks and activities that do not serve you.

INSIDER TIPS

Progress. Manage the doctorate like a project Apply time management principles to complete. Find ways to demonstrate progress. Nominate a peer to act as an accountability partner to aid progress. Say no to unrealistic demands and focus on priorities. Accept that there are times when plans change. Adapt and move on.

INSIDER TIPS

Purposefully file. For instance, a task with no specific deadline goes into a to-do list or task list. A meeting, conversation, event, or task with a specific time or deadline is a calendar appointment. Text or audio goes into a note-taking app. Documents, photos, and videos go into cloud storage. Sensitive items relating to the research are stored in password-protected files and on devices and platforms with two-factor authentication.

Update files and folders weekly. Allocate 45 minutes weekly to sort files, archive materials, and tidy notes. Tag items you want to examine more closely and set up a task to do the work. Tag and archive what you don't need.

Organise according to outcomes. Do you need a folder for articles and resources, research, thesis chapters, or to store raw data? Set up a system that works for you.

Ask: Is it a nice-to-do or a need-to-do item?

SUMMARY

The focus of this chapter was on progress, mindset, and momentum and accepting that some tasks, and indeed the PhD itself, can take longer than expected and, according to the literature, extensions are inevitable. Go with the flow.

Key terms

Completion mindset
Doctoral enablers
Feedback
Fixed Mindset Persona
Growth Mindset

> "You (and your family) are living with the doctorate. Treat it like a friend."
>
> Part-time PhD, Theology

▶ USEFUL RESOURCES AND REFERENCES

References

Byron, K. (2009). *The Creative Researcher, published by The Careers Research and Advisory Centre (CRAC) Limited*. Cambridge.

Dweck, C. S. (2017). *Mindset - Updated edition: Changing the way you think to fulfil your potential* (p. 260). London: Little, Brown Book Group: Kindle Edition: ISBN: 978-1-47213-996-2.

Gonzalez, F. J. (1991). Aristotle on pleasure and perfection. *Phronesis, 36* (2), 141–159. Available at : http://www.jstor.org/stable/4182383

Lerouge, I., & Hoi, T., (2020). *Towards a research integrity culture at universities*. Leuven: LERU publications. Available at: https://www.leru.org/files/Towards-a-Research-Integrity-Culture-at-Universities-full-paper.pdf

Mantai, L. (2019). 'A source of sanity': The role of social support for doctoral candidates' belonging and becoming. *International Journal of Doctoral Studies, 14*, 367–382. https://doi.org/10.28945/4275

Pitchforth, J., Beames, S., Thomas, A., Falk, M., Farr, C., Gasson, S., Thamrin, S. A., & Mengersen, K. (2012). Factors affecting timely completion of a PhD: A complex systems approach. *Journal of the Scholarship of Teaching and Learning, 12* (4), 124–135. Retrieved from: https://scholarworks.iu.edu/journals/index.php/josotl/article/view/3144

Thomas, D. (2016). *The PhD writing handbook* (pp. 175, 177–184). London: Palgrave Macmillan: ISBN: 978-1-137-49769-7.

Tizazu Fetene, G., & Tamrat, W. (2021) *International Journal of Doctoral Studies, 16*, 319–337. https://doi.org/10.28945/4744

van de Schoot, R., Yerkes, M. A., Mouw, J. M., & Sonneveld, H. (2013). What took them so long? Explaining PhD delays among doctoral candidates. *PLoS ONE, 8* (7), e68839. https://journals.plos.org/plosone/article?id=10.1371/journal.pone.0068839

Resources

Raffan, A. (2023). *Knowledge ecology. What percentage of PhD students don't finish?* https://www.knowledgeecology.me/what-percentage-of-phd-students-dont-finish/

Think Post Grads. (2023). *Top 10 tips for PhD completion.* https://www.postgraduatestudentships.co.uk/advice_hub/top-10-tips-for-successful-phd-completion/

Thomas, K. (2014). Finishing your PhD thesis: 15 top tips from those in the know. *Guardian Newspaper, Higher Education Online.* https://www.theguardian.com/higher-education-network/blog/2014/aug/27/finishing-phd-thesis-top-tips-experts-advice

TU Delft. (2019). *Why PhDs are not obtaining their doctorates on time.* https://delta.tudelft.nl/en/article/why-phds-are-not-obtaining-their-doctorates-time

Vitae. (n.d.). *Researcher professional development.* https://www.vitae.ac.uk/

8 Writing and editing

INSIGHTS

"Writing starts with the first word you put on paper. Use writing as a way to sort your ideas so that you are understood."

PhD, Communication

▶ INTRODUCTION

Doctoral candidates stop when they are faced with a long-form writing task such as writing up findings, drafting the thesis and putting their own opinion on the page. At the doctoral level, writing is more than putting words on paper. It is a thoughtful process that requires deep thinking, planning, and belief in yourself to start and time. Undistracted time is needed so you can map your ideas, play with words, and enjoy telling the story of your doctoral research journey and allow the reader to decide whether they accept, challenge, or reject your argument.

Editing and critiquing the work comes later. The focus of writing is to keep going.

DOI: 10.4324/9781003413691-11

▶ WHY CLEAR, CONCISE, AND UNDER-STANDABLE WRITING IS IMPORTANT

The function of a thesis is to ensure that the reader understands the research and its conclusions. It also provides a space for critical evaluation and provides valuable references that underpin arguments in the thesis. The body of work in the first instance will be reviewed by your supervisor/promoter and then by external and internal examiners. It should also be relevant outside of niche scholarly journals and engage with those who choose to adopt, advocate, or challenge the findings. Focus on quality, robustness, and accuracy.

A typical writing process (Table 8.1) consists of putting together a brief, gathering information, reviewing materials, and drafting text. In academia, drafting is subdivided into a pre-write (an

TABLE 8.1 Typical writing process

1. **Brief.**
   What is the task specifically?
   What are the markers for success?
   What is the deadline?
   Do I understand what is expected of me (content, word count, format, etc.)

2. **Gather information. Review materials.**

3. **Pre-write/outline.**
   What are the key elements in the piece?
   Headings? Sub-headings?
   What are the three most important points to make?

4. **Draft text.**

5. **Revise text.**
   Is it in a logical order?
   Are the key points covered?
   Are there any gaps?

6. **Edit text.**
   Does the text need to be condensed, reworded, expanded, or removed?
   Does the text add value to the material?

7. **Format the document.**
   Does it comply with submission guidelines?
   Is the language and tone of voice fit for purpose?
   Is it coherent, logical, and credible?

(Continued)

TABLE 8.1 (Continued)

8. **Check facts, claims, references, spelling, and coherence**
Check that facts, claims, and references are correct and appropriately cited.
Proofread, grammar, and sense check.

9. **Approve content.**
Seek approval and feedback from supervisors/appropriate stakeholders.
Confirm that you can stand over the content and approve it.

10. **Deliver.**
Submit the material for exam, publication, and/or defence.

Typical writing process. © 2023 Sinéad Hewson.

ideation process which highlights the outline, purpose, and key points to be included in a piece of written work), developing a draft, revisions, and editing. It is followed up with a format check, citation and grammar check, and approved before it is delivered and submitted for examination or defence.

Typical writing process

INSIDER TIPS

On writing.

Journal regularly. It acts as a brain dump; it helps sort ideas and gets blurts or intruding thoughts out of your head and onto the page. It can help you re-calibrate, give focus to an idea, and sets the tone for the remainder of the day.

Be patient. It takes longer to write and process material than you think. For instance, an abstract sounds like something that is written quickly. It takes time. An abstract summarises a research paper, thesis, or chapter in 150 to 300 words. It is concise, understandable, makes sense on its own, and is clear. It contains original text, typically in third person past tense.

▶ WRITING AND EDITING

A literature review references articles from disciplines relevant to the doctorate and can contain linguistic biases and sectoral preferences writers adopt to gain acceptance. Established scholars say that candidates should recognise that there is a need to adopt certain language characteristics in their written work and presentations in order to gain authority in their area of expertise.

There can be competing perceptions of importance, value, and relevance between disciplines and siloed working where researching a literature review can highlight similar systems, processes, and conclusions developed in isolation from other areas of expertise. Sometimes a supervisor will recommend a particular approach to this issue or suggest that literature from within rather than outside the area of speciality is cited. Accepting standard convention can be a challenge for non-academic candidates as well as the practise of repeating points within a document, which to a standard reader has no added value. As an author, be open to feedback and consider the best next steps that allow you to progress AND showcase the key points and insights in the literature review.

Some academics argue that dense language comes with the territory. They say that some level of difficulty and struggle is essential to develop understanding of an argument, concept, or proposal. It is useful when writing to examine whether complicated language and terms can help demonstrate your expertise and knowledge rather than promote understanding for the reader (Thomas, 2016). My advice is that the purpose of the literature review is to share current thinking and include information that enables the user to critically analyse a specific research topic.

The linguistic heritage of a specialist area is useful to understand as the doctorate progresses, paying special attention to word usage, accuracy, language quality, and context. This can help you find your academic voice. It is something which will continue to evolve even when the PhD is complete. Ensure that language choice is clear, concise, and understandable. Identify and capture valuable words, phrases, and concepts that you can use and try to write in a way that your message is crystal clear in any context. There are academics, researchers, and experts who struggle to be understood outside of their specialist area, mature candidates and those who work outside of academia can share knowledge, insights, and critical thinking skills beyond scholarly circles.

Academia values the process of unpicking, exploring, and restructuring a concept. For example, you may have developed text for a presentation or paper, and it has been well received. What would happen if you examined the content from a different point of view? Examination through different lenses can convert complex issues into concise, comprehendible information chunks. Effectiveness increases further when combined with a clear call to action.

Decision-making (what to keep and delete)

Academic authors face multiple decisions on how to explore, discuss, and address their research question. First of all, they need to establish criteria for data selection and inclusion before primary research data can be analysed, explored, and presented. They then have to decide on the inclusion and exclusion of data based on the research aims and nature of the findings. Then, they articulate information that is new, unexpected, or significant within their area of expertise.

The relevance of specific data sets to address the research question and suitable ways to present the material is key so that "key findings" are presented "in context" and as a "logical series of breakdowns" in order to facilitate analysis, discussion, and highlight important research points without "overwhelming" the reader (Denscombe, 1998). Identifying display formats appropriate to the purpose of the study shed light on how much data can be reported and summarised without changing its nature and meaning (Dey, 1993). This step acts as a signpost for information placement in a dissertation, within a chapter, as an appendix, or exclusion from the thesis.

Management of expectations when presenting the data is important and should consider the researcher, participant, supervisor, and reader's perspective. This means being absolutely clear in the research when or if new material is presented, combined with a focus on quality and determination to do the data justice and treating sensitive information with care (Tracy, 2010).

Pattern identification involves applying key themes that emerge from the data and can influence the final data analysis. An emergent approach ensures that the voice of the participant rather than the assumptions of the researcher shape the findings and the final version of the data discussion/analysis and synthesis chapter. In the end, you can discuss with your supervisor and peers and identify which tone of voice is most appropriate to tell the research story.

Arguments and logical fallacies

Doctoral candidates play a significant role in shaping academic research, innovation, and the creation of new ideas. Their main objective is to conduct thorough research on a specific topic, challenge assumptions, establish new perspectives, and contribute to scholarly discourse. This requires extensive investigation, data collection and evaluation, and the formation of clear academic arguments.

Academic opinion is presented within a series of clear academic arguments that start with a claim or hypothesis, use logical reasoning, and present verifiable evidence to support the claim. Since arguments are subject to counterclaims and rebuttals, it is important that researchers at this advanced level have the resilience, skill set, and know-how to meet these intellectual challenges head-on and deliver robust, truthful work (Rose, 2017; Sesonske, 1968; Tandoc et al., 2018).

What is an argument?

Arguments can be strong or weak. Strong arguments are logical, truth-based, and robust while weak arguments use logical fallacies and flawed logic to appear stronger than they actually are. A logical fallacy is an argument that can be disproved using reasoning and is logically flawed or deceptive in some way.

Logical fallacies and the selective use of information can unite, divide, and polarise, while communication that contradicts and lacks clarity creates confusion and mistrust. Sometimes logical fallacies are intentionally used to simplify an issue or make something appear worse or better than it actually is. They can also be unintentional. This occurs when an argument is not thought through, or there is no awareness that an argument or standpoint is logically flawed.

The easiest way for academics to avoid using logical fallacies is to present work that is well-balanced, objective, and clear. This means carefully considering every point, claim, or comment to support the work with facts and data from credible sources and explaining the rationale behind a decision, finding, or recommendation. Check for contradictions and separate strong ideas from weak ones. Verify how an argument is validated. Link claims, arguments, and thought processes to support, validate, or invalidate a hypothesis and explain why. Remember, this is a work in progress. Things change, and updates are ongoing.

What is a logical fallacy?

A logical fallacy is a convincing argument that appears credible even though it contains flawed reasoning, mistaken beliefs, as well as invalid or illogical arguments. Fallacies occur when arguments are not fully thought through or when there is no recognition that an argument is logically flawed. The majority of fallacies are accidental.

Doctorates, arguments and logical fallacies

Individuals who have been away from academia express concern about the robustness of their writing. The following section uses the concepts of arguments and logical fallacies. It is designed to help readers self-evaluate the strengths and weaknesses of their content, ideas, presentation, and writing style.

Glossary of fallacies

Ad hominem fallacy

An ad hominem fallacy is a personal attack that undermines an opponent citing irrelevant personal traits instead of logic to counteract an argument. For example, claiming that John is eligible for a role because he is 15 years older than the rest of the team.

TIP: When reviewing text, ask: Does the material personally attack or undermine someone based on a personal trait or fact?

Ambiguity

Ambiguity involves the use of words or phrases that can be interpreted in different ways (amphiboly), imply two distinct meanings (equivocation), or when a sentence to explain a context is missing. For instance, the joke, A man walks into a bar. "Ouch!" is an example of ambiguity. It can be used with the intent to confuse, mislead, or misrepresent a context or with the aim of concealing an argument's weakness.

TIP: When reviewing material, ask: Is the message clear? Does the text make sense? Is it coherent, logical, and universally understood?

Anecdotal

The use of personal experience or an isolated example to support a claim *instead* of presenting a valid argument is called an anecdote. For example: "My aunt said she has more energy since going vegan. This means that plant-based diets reduce fatigue symptoms."

TIP: When presenting material ask: Is this an evidence-based argument? What is the source? When an anecdote is used to illustrate a point, it should be explicitly stated as such.

Appeal to authority

Appeal to authority relies on the opinion or involvement of an authority figure or institution to validate a statement instead of a logical argument. It occurs when expertise is overstated, irrelevant, or false. For instance, stating that "television exposure significantly influencing feline health and wellbeing is validated by Nobel Economics laureate and pedigree cat owner Professor Jones who agreed in an interview that it is true" is an example of an appeal to authority.

TIP: When reviewing material, ask: Does this source add value to the piece? Is the source credible and relevant to the work? What is the reason for using this citation (is it because it looks good or because it is relevant)?

Appeal to emotion

Appeal to emotion (arguing through feelings) is using an emotional response instead of a valid argument to make a point. For example, "the government must establish a legal framework limiting screen time nationwide. Think of the significant impact it will have on children worldwide".

TIP: When reviewing material ask: Is this a fact-based comment or an emotionally driven point? If an appeal to emotion is used, does its use strengthen or weaken the argument?

Appeal to hypocrisy/tu quoque fallacy

Appeal to hypocrisy is a reactive response that uses criticism or hypocrisy to counteract a point rather than addressing the claim itself. For example, when someone says "You are not qualified to talk about ethical standards" and the response is "Neither are you".

TIP: When on the receiving end of this type of comment, take the opportunity to deliver a thoughtful, well-considered response, rather than a hastily drafted reply. Use the situation to demonstrate respect, expertise, and know-how.

Appeal to ignorance/burden of proof fallacy

The appeal to ignorance fallacy is also known as the burden of proof fallacy. It claims that something is true (or false) because there is a lack of contrary evidence saying otherwise. For instance, a project leader might hire colleagues for a research project without concrete evidence of approval, claiming that if the proposal were denied, the committee would have informed them by now.

TIP: To avoid this error, ask: Is the argument or decision based on an assumption? Does the evidence clearly validate the claim or proposed action?

Appeal to nature

The appeal to nature fallacy suggests that natural means that something is good, justified, or better than something unnatural. For example, a marketing campaign might say that grass-fed beef is healthier than lab-grown beef because it is a natural product without any evidence to justify the claim.

TIP: When reviewing material, ask: Does the argument rely on the assumption that natural is always better? If so, is there credible supporting evidence in the text? Is it clearly referenced?

Appeal to pity/ad misericordiam

Appeal to pity uses emotion to gain sympathy to support an argument instead of factual evidence. It is also called an ad misericordiam fallacy. For instance, a colleague might push for co-authorship on a paper you lead and say: "If you say no, I will lose my place on the doctoral programme and end up jobless".

TIP: Stay on track and focus on the facts to determine the next steps, and seek guidance from a trustworthy colleague or supervisor.

Bandwagon fallacy

The bandwagon fallacy assumes something is true because it is popular. If everyone thinks this way, accept the status quo or miss out. Popularity does not mean the argument is evidenced, logical, or justified. For example, a research colleague might secure the nomination for a leadership position simply because they are well-known on campus; however, this does not necessarily mean they are the most suitable candidate for the role.

TIP: When reviewing material, it is important to consider whether including an argument based on popularity is relevant, credible, and justified.

Begging the question

Begging the question, also known as petitio principii or a circular argument, is a fallacy that presents a logically sounding argument. It assumes that the conclusion is true without evidence to support it. For example, when someone advises against reading a journal because it's a waste of time, it may be a begging-the-question fallacy because there is no credible justification for why this is the case.

TIP: To avoid this fallacy, ask clarifying questions to understand the reasoning behind a claim.

Black or white

A black-or-white fallacy, also known as an either/or dilemma, occurs when two options are given, even though a number of credible alternatives are possible. For example, a researcher might contend that stakeholder analysis identifies an individual as pro-vaccination or anti-vaccination while other patterns might exist.

TIP: To avoid this fallacy when reviewing data, consider whether there are convincing alternatives in addition to either/or options.

Burden of proof

Burden of proof is an informal fallacy which occurs when the requirement to demonstrate and validate a claim with credible evidence is unconvincing or inappropriate. It is based on the premise that something is true unless proven otherwise. For example, if there is a claim that the level of innovation proposed in a project is breakthrough, the burden of proof is on the party making the claim to clearly demonstrate that it is indeed a first-of-a-kind innovation that transforms entire markets, industries or creates new ones.

TIP: When reviewing data and drafting research findings, ask, is this information, evidence-based and relevant to the study? Is it presented in a clear and convincing manner? Does it credibly support the claim?

Causal fallacy

A causal fallacy incorrectly relates a cause to an effect, when in fact the relationship does not exist or cannot be proven. It is also known as questionable cause. For instance, saying that the sale of sleeping bags increases when music festival acts are confirmed, therefore the headline act is the cause of increased sales, is an example of a causal fallacy.

TIP: When reviewing material, verify that arguments are logical and sound. Confirm that the text is correct and supported by credible, referenced sources. Ask: Is the claim accurate and clearly stated? Does the material explain how the conclusion was reached? Are there any errors or gaps that need to be addressed?

Circular argument

A circular argument is a fallacy where the premise and conclusion are the same. The argument is illogical and fails to justify or provide supporting evidence to validate a claim. An example of a circular argument is a statement such as "The expert panel is right because they are the experts".

TIP: When reviewing material, critically review the construction of arguments and claims. Are they logical and well thought through? Is the claim clear, and is the evidence supporting the conclusion justified?

Composition

The fallacy of composition assumes that the truth about one part of something can be applied to the entire thing. For instance, the statement "if a family saves money by spending less and reduces their debt by taking extra work, then the entire economy can also save more money by spending less and reduce debt by working longer hours" is an example of composition fallacy.

TIP: To avoid this error, critically evaluate and be accountable for the accuracy, relevance and robustness of your work.

Division

The fallacy of division assumes that the truth about an entire thing can be applied to all of its parts. A common example is to assume that all singers are wealthy because the highest-paid musician is a singer.

TIP: When reviewing material, take responsibility for its accuracy and assess the quality of the content.

Equivocation

Equivocation is characterised by unclear phrasing, wordplay, as well as the use words with multiple meanings. It occurs when language confuses, misleads, or deceives so that an argument has a different interpretation to what is actually said. For example, when someone asks "is there a doctor in the house?" they are looking for a medical professional, not a PhD.

TIP: When reviewing material, consider rephrasing arguments, provide examples, factual evidence, and explain how the conclusion was reached. Be clear and validate the work.

Fallacy fallacy

Fallacy fallacy assumes that a conclusion is invalid because there is an error of reasoning within a poorly constructed argument. However, flawed reasoning does not necessarily mean that this is the case. For example, a study might suggest that adults should take a daily walk because it is free and refreshing, while someone else might argue that adults should sleep every day for the same reasons.

TIP: To properly review material, it is important to focus on the logic and reasoning of the argument, as well as the credibility and accuracy of the conclusion.

False dilemma/dichotomy

False dilemma is a fallacy because it limits understanding of a situation by presenting only two options. It is also known as a false dichotomy and can be used to force a decision or polarise groups. For example, when someone takes a "my way or the highway" approach to a critical decision, they create a false dilemma by not considering other reasonable alternatives.

TIP: To avoid false dilemmas, it is important to acknowledge that there are other options besides the proposed ones and to justify the rationale for proposing only two alternatives.

Gambler's fallacy

Gambler's fallacy or maturity of chances is built on flawed reasoning that the next outcome of a statistically independent event is more or less likely to occur based on prior results. For instance, in roulette if the ball lands on the same colour ten times in a row, gambler's fallacy would propose that the ball is more likely to land on another colour. However, this is not the case. This form of flawed reasoning is also known as the Monte Carlo fallacy.

TIP: To avoid this fallacy, consider whether a particular task is a statistically independent event and demonstrate why this is the case.

Genetic

Genetic fallacy occurs when an argument is accepted or rejected based upon the source of information or who it is from rather than the content itself. It occurs when there is confusion between reasons and causes, psychological and logical explanations, and sources and arguments. For instance, a committee not approving a proposed research methodology because the author is a consultant, not an academic, is an example of a genetic fallacy. This is because the information source has no bearing on the robustness of the methods applied in the research.

TIP: When reviewing material, focus on the argument, its premise, the evidence, and the reasoning behind an argument rather than the source. Ask: Is the argument sound and well formulated, and does the conclusion have clear evidence to support it?

Hasty generalisation

The hasty generalisation or over-generalisation fallacy occurs when a claim is made based on evidence that inadequately supports the claim because it is too small. The argument is poorly reasoned because the conclusion is based on limited data. It can also occur when sufficient research or sample size in one area is deemed inadequate in another. For instance, an example of over-generalisation is when a report says that 25% of working men in Amsterdam Zuid share the household burden with their female counterparts and concludes that 75% of men across Europe do not help with household chores.

TIP: When reviewing material, rework content so that it is logically sound. This means understanding the scale and scope of data sources and adapting work to reflect the evidence rather than vice versa.

Loaded question

A loaded or trick question contains an unverified assumption that can result in a damaging response and undermine credibility. The tactic can be used in scenario planning and in research defence meetings to assess the robustness and preparedness of a strategy, while tabloid media tend to use loaded questions to generate a story.

TIP: When confronted with a loaded question, determine whether the intention is to provoke a reaction or if is it a poorly constructed question. Rephrase the question and respond by addressing the presupposition and flawed reasoning. It is also possible to refuse to answer the question and explain why.

Middle ground

The middle ground fallacy is an error in reasoning which proposes that a solution always lies between two opposing arguments. It is also known as false equivalence, argument to moderation, and the golden mean fallacy. An example of this is when a scientist adopts the middle ground in their findings while the evidence clearly validates one of the opposing arguments, resulting in a misleading conclusion.

TIP: When reviewing material, it is important to critically examine the evidence and determine whether a compromise is necessary. Identify the consequences of an evidence-based recommendation versus one adopting the middle ground.

No true Scotsman

No true Scotsman, also known as the appeal to purity fallacy, is a flawed argument containing vague generalisations to characterise a group based on the behaviours of an individual or group subset. No true Scotsman proposes that those who do not share these characteristics are not really part of the group. For instance, someone might argue that vegans who use flypaper are not vegan because a true vegan would never kill a fly.

TIP: When reviewing material, check that all statements are supported with credible, verifiable evidence and that sources are clearly cited.

Personal incredulity

Personal incredulity is a fallacy which occurs when a valid argument is rejected or hard to believe because it is difficult to comprehend, there is lack of knowledge, or it is misunderstood. For example, someone might discount an important study because the subject is complex and hard to follow rather than examining the findings and checking whether the research recommendations are valid.

TIP: When counteracting personal incredulity, ask clarifying questions and provide evidence and clearly referenced sources demonstrating that the feedback is not justified.

Red herring fallacy

A red herring is an attempt to shift focus by introducing an irrelevant or unimportant point, fact, idea, or event towards something which is safer or easier to address. The fallacy aims to confuse, distract, or shift attention away from a topic and towards a false conclusion. It can be intentional or unintentional. For example, someone might say: "The team missed Friday's funding deadline, but the conference presentation received a standing ovation last week. It was a fantastic example of teamwork".

TIP: When reviewing material, ask, is this point necessary? Is it credible? Is it relevant and does it add value?

Slippery slope fallacy

The slippery slope fallacy argues that taking a specific action sets off a chain of unsubstantiated events that ultimately result in an extreme or absurd outcome. Once started, events increase in severity and are difficult to stop. An example of a slippery slope is when someone says if the journal article is rejected, then everyone will think the study has failed. Then, before you know it, the funding is gone, and we will be destitute.

TIP: When addressing a slippery slope argument, it is important to point out that the events are not necessarily connected and to provide evidence that a different outcome is possible.

Special pleading

Special pleading or moving the goalposts is a fallacy that seeks exemption from a rule or behaviour that is expected of everyone else without reasonable justification. It is a fallacy that is easier to identify in others and typically based on emotion rather than facts. For instance, it is a double standard to agree that breaching clinical standards warrants disciplinary action, and then argue that a particular case is different and should not be punished.

TIP: To mitigate the risk of special pleading, understand and adhere to the standards in your area of study. When a potential double standard is identified, ask clarifying questions, take steps, and provide evidence to address the issue.

Straw man argument

The straw man fallacy is an error of reasoning where someone's point of view is misrepresented by an opponent so that it is easier to refute and undermine. Moreover, a different issue to the one in hand is addressed so that a more convenient alternative is proposed. For instance, when someone says that an independent expert is only focused on promoting their own interests rather than the wider impact of a research proposal, straw man tactics such as oversimplification, taking things out of context, or cherry-picking which areas to focus on are used to make the point.

TIP: To avoid this fallacy, focus on researching and understanding the issue as well as knowing the opponents' point of view. Before responding, it is also useful to clarify whether their opinion is a misunderstanding or an attempt to undermine or garner support.

Sunk cost fallacy

A sunk cost fallacy justifies a particular course of action even though the additional costs outweigh the benefits. For instance, when someone says that they will continue using a citation tool even though it does not perform as expected because of the time and effort inputting references and learning how to use it.

TIP: To address this fallacy, critically assess the return on investment (RoI) of a proposed action and seek objective feedback. Ask: Is this the best use of time, money, and resources?

Texas sharpshooter

The Texas sharpshooter, also known as the clustering illusion, is a fallacy that cherry-picks or falsely detects data patterns from randomly distributed samples in an attempt to make sense of something or validate a claim. In research, it can appear when analysis is biased towards data similarities and data differences are not examined.

TIP: To avoid the sharpshooter fallacy, analyse and present data objectively. Citing findings that support and discount the research question and whether the research and its findings are repeatable in a separate study.

▶ LONG-FORM WRITING

Long-form writing should be treated with the same level of detail as planning for a marathon. If you are a beginner, you might join a local Start to Run programme, follow an established programme, or seek specialised support. Then, as you get a feel for the technique, fitness improves, and confidence increases, you push yourself further and grow. Pacing is important: too much or not enough training impacts the quality of the results. This holds for writing, data analysis, and pretty much any activity requiring deep thinking or concentration.

> "If you stress and worry about being a writer ... you are a real writer."
>
> Novelist, former PhD proofreader

Writing, specifically academic writing after time away from academia, overwhelms some and invigorates others. When life gets in the way, and our responsibilities take over the thinking time we seek to write that perfect paragraph, it can generate a sense of overwhelm, creative blocks, and sometimes resentment.

Few people recognise the time we need for deep thinking to process the information, ideas, and new knowledge brewing within. For those of us living in the real world who speak English as a second, third, or fourth language, there can be pressure to write perfectly all the time rather than putting the essence of an idea on the page.

In the draft stage, it's about key points, getting ideas on the page and getting into the flow. Quite often, we find that during the editing process, copious pages condense to one line, a single concept, or can be deleted.

Verbosity and language choice

I'm a plain speaker and an accurate writer. Yet, I feel a sense of irritation and frustration when I read material and have to look up the meaning of words I don't understand especially when a simpler phrase or term would have more impact.

For example, in sociology, a dyad is a group of two people, the smallest possible social group. When I came across the word dyad for the first time and looked up the definition, my brain said "pair" and I questioned why I would use dyad. In my area of expertise the word "pair" was appropriate.

As you progress, focus on language quality. Consider adopting plain language and avoid "verbose" or convoluted language, jargon, euphemisms, and ambiguous language (Bloomberg, 2023).

When I write, my first drafts are verbose, and I focus on the key points, putting text on the pages. Then, I edit and polish the wording. I tested Grammarly and the Magic Write function on Canva to AI to see if they improve the structure of written text. They can rephrase, adjust the tone, and expand or shorten text; however, the text produced is not necessarily original. It is your responsibility as a writer to check for accuracy and plagiarism. Although these tools are useful for generic items such as an email, invitation format or to suggest an alternative phrase or word, they are not mature enough (yet) to generate specialist text or incorporate the critical thinking capabilities of a PhD candidate. The ideas come from you, and minor text edits can be refined with AI. If you use AI tools, say so.

> "When I rewrote the thesis, about 40 pages of the original remained. Each sentence was focused, and I asked – does this reflect the data, is it adding value / enriching / proving new thoughts, dialogue and discussion?"
>
> Part-time PhD, Communication

▶ WRITING TO ESTABLISH A CREDIBLE ACADEMIC VOICE

Clear writing demonstrating academic credibility takes time, effort, and careful consideration. It is built on well-constructed, purposeful arguments that are properly referenced and easy to understand. Refinement comes later. It is not unusual for candidates to feel vulnerable presenting early drafts for peer review or when established academics critique their work. This step towards completion affords the opportunity to reflect, refine arguments, perfect the text, and deliver a robust body of work that potentially contributes to new knowledge.

In search of academic authenticity

> "I wish I'd known what I was letting myself in for. Not just the workload but the culture, the etiquette and group dynamics. I needed to change my terminology from a consultant to an academic one."
>
> PhD, Social Sciences

Academic writing consists of a variety of subject-specific literacies. It seeks to present ideas that make the most sense to readers. This involves, in part, adopting an appropriate identity to connect with the reader. The goal of any written material presented as part of a doctorate is to present a robust body of work that is accurate, accessible, and provokes thought. Mindful word choice facilitates the deeper exploration of a research topic. Academic turns of phrase which do not add to the conversation should be avoided.

If you are unsure about your writing and communication skills, consider the habits of non-native English speakers; they are careful with word choice. When they write, they aim to be accurate, and authentic, and communicate clearly in order to minimise misunderstandings. Academic literature highlights the difficulties international groups have with native English speakers, noting that complex word choice can confuse rather than clarify.

Useful examples of clear writing include the *The Creative Researcher*, published by The Careers Research and Advisory Centre (CRAC) Limited (Byron 2009), the Plain English Campaign and Letters Live websites. Some authors use international English or language formats such as plain English and Globish (Global English), which consists of 1500 words with exactly the same meaning in different cultures (Norris, 2013). There has been a call in some circles to expand and include scientific phrases so that research terms are universally understood. The Plain English Campaign website also has a function offering the plain English example of a word, for example, the word "moreover" is used in academic writing to connect points, and the site proposes plain English alternatives such as "and, also" and "as well".

▶ WRITING TIPS

"I adopted a different writing style aligned with my area of expertise. It involved culling reams of copy into short, sharp sentences. Over time, I was discerning in my presentation of the state of the art, and a ruthless side emerged, deciding what could stay or be deleted from my final thesis. This was an important aspect of the doctoral experience."

Part-time research PhD

Initially, you may feel that you are wading through the literature and struggling to get the words on the page. Playing rather than agonising over a sentence helps to get something on paper and focus. If you cannot find the words, send an email or voicemail to yourself clarifying a point and do so in the style of a particular author, newsreader, or pundit. Question the material, its purpose, relevance, and place in the final dissertation. If you were the leading expert in your field, how to present the state of the art to peers? Over time, your critical, discerning academic voice will emerge, and its focus will be to provoke thought through quality and communication. (See Table 8.2 for tips.)

TABLE 8.2 Ten writing habit tips

1. Some writers deep dive into a project, while others use chunks of time to work.
2. Write one page at a time.
3. Write daily, even if it is just for 15 mins.
4. Read. It helps you become a better researcher. Identify well-written stories by reputable authors/academics in the sector (Bloomberg and Volpe, 2008).
5. Play with writing styles and experiment with your academic voice.
6. Pay attention to patterns, insights and the unusual – notice what you are noticing.
7. Write it down – on paper, with technology ... note your observations (pen & paper, Evernote, Scrivener, voice record, send an email, SMS, or WhatsApp to yourself). Set up an ideas and carpark list.
8. Write now – edit later ... Cull later.
9. Write about what you love. When you are passionate about your subject matter, it bursts through in the thesis tone of voice and how you show up and present and answer questions at the viva. It is authentic.
10. Write, let the words flow – then take time to review. Some experienced academics say that writing is the easy part. The hard bit is planning and organising the material into useful chunks of information that add value to the body of work.

Ten Writing Habit Tips. © 2023 Sinéad Hewson.

Ten writing habit tips

As you analyse the data and start writing your dissertation, be aware that your opinion on how the material should be presented will change. For example, an *Analysis and Synthesis* chapter might start as a linear chapter following a standard format – this is what we wanted to do, this is what we did, and this is what we found out. As the material develops, this type of format might not fully reflect the value of the work and the content might evolve into a series of emerging ideas for the reader to examine.

Practise makes perfect: Play with your writing and presentation style. Practise and learn from it. Read the work of opinion leaders and activists in your area of specialisation. Observe and listen to podcasts, interviews, and conference presentations. Prepare and record a presentation or write an article using their tone of voice, gestures, and word patterns and notice what resonates with you. Ask what aspects of these articles, interviews, or presentations can help me develop my academic voice and move me towards completion. Consider this approach when preparing for presentations, practising questions, and preparing for the viva or thesis defence.

To improve writing. The more you write, the less intimidating writing seems to be. Practise writing skills by writing a series of article notes adopting the writing style of someone you admire academically in your field. Then, adjust the piece to your own writing style. Reflect on what you like and don't like and get out of your comfort zone.

Effective feedback on written work. Tips for success

When reviewing written work, take the perspective of a reader with little or no knowledge of the topic or the author. Be pragmatic, honest, and kind.

Consider the following questions to guide the feedback:

1. Is the material logical, coherent, and relevant?
2. Are the key points and central arguments relevant and consistent with the current state of the art?
3. Is the text clear and easy to understand?
4. Does the text add value and inform the reader's understanding of the topic?
5. Is the piece informative, enjoyable to read, and worth including in the body of work?

Constructive, thorough feedback improves the quality of writing and academic output (Dweck, 2017). It is a positive step towards completion.

Exercise: Playing with writing styles

Step 1   2–4 hours

Pick three doctoral dissertations in your specialist area (https://ethos.bl.uk/ or Arrow@TU Dublin – the research repository of Technological University Dublin). Briefly review the introduction, literature review, and closing chapters. Using the guiding questions from the literature review notes template (Table 6.1. Taking notes for a literature review), identify three characteristics of the author's writing style that can help develop your academic voice.

Step 2   Duration 45–180 minutes

Take a random page from one of the dissertations and draft your version of the text. Reflect on how this informs your writing style.

We are at our most vulnerable when we write. These words come from our souls whether we articulate findings from quantitative or qualitative data. It is important to be familiar with and follow the language taxonomy of your specialty area.

The initial stage of writing is about getting your ideas on the page. I used flip-chart paper and home office wall was covered with a chart for each thesis chapter. As the writing evolved ten chapters merged into five.

> "Sometimes it's an achievement if I write 100 words a day. When I have a deadline, I can churn 1,000, 5,000, even 10,000 words a day."
>
> Novelist, former PhD proofreader

Tips for when I don't understand

At doctoral level, expertise and knowledge is demonstrated with the use of accurate terms, concise language, and well-constructed arguments. As a mature, part-time candidate with industry experience, internal pressure to be the expert, to be correct can reach a crisis when you come across a term you do not understand (Mantai, 2019).

Useful tips to assess whether the phrase is important for the research is to:

1. Access existing glossaries to find out their meaning.
2. Set up a glossary file with definitions, terms, and phrases that are useful for the research.
3. Explain the term in plain English (so that an 11-year-old would understand) in a way that is both professional and relatable to the average reader.
4. Ask for clarification on usage if your supervisor or peer uses a complex phrase. Check that your interpretation is appropriate by saying something like "so what you mean is …".
5. Read, engage with, and follow thought leaders and peers in your field. Notice how they express themselves verbally and in writing. Is there a style or approach that you would like to adopt, or will you develop your own academic voice?
6. Write a sample piece of text for your dissertation with the phrase to demonstrate understanding.

Tips to bullet-proof your work

1. Start by reading other people's work and recognise what makes a good argument.
2. When a statement or claim is made in your work, ask the question: "according to whom?"
3. Find, check, and verify the original sources cited in your work.
4. Perceptual positions. When reviewing material, draft text, or claims. Review the material a number of times from different perspectives, namely the reader (who does not know you), your supervisor, your examiner, someone who is opposed to your point of view, and yourself. Ask: What do I want the reader to know, understand, and consider? What does the reader/supervisor examiner/or antagonist need to know, understand, and consider? Use these insights to strengthen the quality of your work and to address areas that require further editing, clarity, or removal.
5. If you find logical fallacies in your work, be kind to yourself. Identifying a fallacy is an opportunity to strengthen and present the body of work in a robust and coherent manner.

> "Measure twice, cut once. Write, edit, revise, revise, submit."
> Part-time PhD, Communication

Exercise: Connect back to the why

Reflect on the prospect of writing proposals articles, writing up results, and drafting the thesis. Does having an academic voice motivate you? Does it fulfil the "why am I doing this?" driver identified in the motivation chapter. What changes (if any) will you propose to align the communication, writing, and editing tasks with your values? What needs to change, you or the research? Ask: In what ways can I demonstrate excellence through my writing, presentations, and talks?

Exercise: Integrate into the work plan

Review the Typical writing process (Table 8.1), and consider how you will develop and grow your writing and review capabilities, bit by bit. Integrate this into the work plan.

Reflect: have I taken a SMART (specific, measurable, realistic, and timely) approach to the work? Commit and allocate (undisturbed) time in your agenda to complete the work. Keep it simple and include breaks and time to write and reflect on the messages you want to communicate.

Closing thought

Writing is the vehicle that makes your ideas tangible and exposes your work to a wider audience. Focus on what you want them to know about the work, the research process, and your conclusions. Enjoy the process.

▶ SUMMARY

This chapter emphasises the importance of writing and developing an academic voice. It went through a typical writing process with the aim of embedding a behaviour that writing is a joyful way to express ideas and demonstrate excellence. The literature suggests the effort required to present the work coherently in written form increases the risk of stopping; the aim of the chapter was to unpick the process and build confidence and self-belief that writing is the key to completion and a strong defence.

Key terms

Arguments and logical fallacies
Completion Mindset
Editing
Feedback

Writing tips
Writing process

> "If you worry about writing, you are an author."
> Author, former thesis editor

▶ USEFUL RESOURCES AND REFERENCES

References

Bloomberg, L. D. (2023) *Completing your qualitative dissertation: A road map from beginning to end.* London: SAGE Publications. Kindle Edition: ISBN: 978-1-0718-6981-9.

Bloomberg, L. D., and Volpe, M. (2008). *Completing your qualitative dissertation: A roadmap from beginning to end. Part 1: Taking charge of yourself and your work.* Sage Publications. doi:10.4135/978145 2226613

Denscombe, M. (1998). *The good research guide for small scale social research projects* (p. 191). Buckingham: Open University Press: ISBN: 0335198066. Available at: https://archive.org/details/goodresearch guid00dens_0/page/182/mode/2up/search/overload

Dey, I. (1993). *Qualitative data analysis: A user-friendly guide for social scientists* (pp. 85, 103, 201, 250). New York: Routledge: ISBN: 9780203412497.

Dweck, C. S. (2017). *Mindset - Updated edition: Changing the way you think to fulfil your potential* (p. 260). London: Little, Brown Book Group. Kindle Edition: ISBN: 978-1-47213-996-2.

Mantai, L. (2019). 'A source of sanity': The role of social support for doctoral candidates' belonging and becoming. *International Journal of Doctoral Studies, 14,* 367–382. doi:10.28945/4275

Norris, V. (2013). Scientific Globish: Clear enough is good enough. *Trends in Microbiology, 21* (10), 503–504. doi:10.1016/j.tim.2013.07. 002. PMID: 24094815.

Rose, J. (2017). Brexit, Trump, and post-truth politics. *Public Integrity, 19* (6), 555–558. doi: 10.1080/10999922.2017.1285540

Sesonske, A. (1968). To make the weaker argument defeat the stronger. *Journal of the History of Philosophy, 6* (3), 217–231. doi:10.1353/ hph.2008.0984

Tandoc, E.C., Lim, Z.W., and Ling, R. (2018). Defining "Fake News". *Digital Journalism, 6* (2), 137–153, doi:10.1080/21670811.2017. 1360143

Byron, K. (2009). *The creative researcher, published by the Careers Research and Advisory Centre (CRAC) limited.* Cambridge. https://www.vitae.ac.uk/vitae-publications/guides-briefings-and-information/vitae-researcher-booklets

Thomas, D. (2016). *The PhD writing handbook* (pp. 175, 177–184). London: Palgrave Macmillan: ISBN: 978-1-137-49769-7.

Tracy, S. J. (2010). Qualitative quality: Eight a "big-tent" criteria for excellent qualitative research. *Qualitative Inquiry, 16* (10), 837–851. doi:10.1177/1077800410383121

A selection of useful resources

Grammarly Blog. *What is the hasty generalization fallacy?* https://www.grammarly.com/blog/hasty-generalization-fallacy/

Plain English Campaign website. https://www.plainenglish.co.uk/services/crystal-mark.html

Purdue University Logical Fallacies. https://owl.purdue.edu/owl/general_writing/academic_writing/logic_in_argumentative_writing/fallacies.html

Stanford University Fallacies. https://plato.stanford.edu/entries/fallacies/-CorFal

University of Kansas, The Writing Process. https://writing.ku.edu/writing-process

University of Manchester, Academic Phrase Bank. https://www.phrasebank.manchester.ac.uk/

Vitae: Researcher professional development. https://www.vitae.ac.uk/

9 Staying on track and deadlines

INSIGHTS

"Make a plan. Update the plan. Stick to the plan."
Part-time PhD candidate, History

▶ INTRODUCTION

Staying on track and meeting deadlines is the focus of this chapter. Even though most doctorates do not complete on time, many candidates feel inadequate, a sense of failure, and frustration when a deadline slips. Multiple factors can be at play, such as the absence of an up-to-date work plan and not understanding where you are in the process. It also includes being pulled in multiple directions and unable to complete a task because there are too many distractions, a lack of a dedicated doctoral workspace, or no energy left to concentrate and focus.

Practical issues such as staying on track, deadlines, timeliness, and adaptability are covered in this section. In addition, helpful strategies, tools, and insights are shared; they are focused on

DOI: 10.4324/9781003413691-12

completion and aim to help candidates recognise when to stop, start, or change direction. This helps set the context for the following chapter, which addresses feedback and setbacks. Remember, finished is better than perfect!

▶ STAYING ON TRACK

Incrementally build success

In order to succeed, understand what is expected of you. Make a plan and stick to it. Focus on managing your time, building a support system, organising well and clear writing.

I researched multiple resources and conducted interviews on the theme of doctoral completion. Mature and part-time candidates undergo a rigorous application process before they are accepted. An external examiner and supervisor interviewed suggested that the system for part-time external candidates is not keeping up with their needs or is patchy in their support. Highly capable individuals drop out because they are not fully prepared for the scale of commitment (10–20 hours a week), work, and attention to detail that is expected. Motivation and truly believing that this is the right thing to do is what keeps you going (Kouzes and Posner, 2018).

A typical doctorate takes up to seven years to complete, and it is unrealistic to remain engaged and fully motivated throughout. Falling out of love with your doctorate is a universal experience, so on the days when things are not going well, take a break from your studies. Switch off and relax. When you return, remind yourself why you are putting yourself through this, find ways to fall in love with the doctorate again, and commit to finishing your studies.

Franklin University in the US cites ten struggles that part-time doctoral candidates face. They are personal isolation, stress, supervisor conflict, funding, time management, work-life balance, lack of institutional support, lack of personal support, concerns about the future, and motivation. They also say that successful candidates have clear priorities, know how to delegate, work normal hours, turn up (even when they don't want to), have a strong sense of purpose, have a designated workspace, and honour themselves. They make time to celebrate, they exercise, they ask for support and help, and create accountability (Dweck, 2017; Mantai 2019).

Does that mean if I fail – that I am not fully committed? I believe that committed candidates falter when the systems they have in place are not suitable for the job or they are inconsistent in their approach to the work. The literature highlights that breaking down the work into smaller pieces works. Plainly put, if you have a clear sense of purpose, organise yourself well, build a support system, write clearly and coherently, and have an overriding sense of purpose – you can complete. This links back to motivation, organisation, process, and self-care (Covey, 2004; Thomas, 2016; Clear, 2018). Those interviewed for the book said that investing time and money to get organised pays off in the longer term.

Own the process – there is always something to do

> ### INSIGHTS
>
> Q: How do you eat an elephant?
> A: Bit by bit.

The key to completing your doctorate is to proactively own and drive your activity programme. There are times when academic systems labour slowly compared to other sectors of society. While you are waiting for feedback, focus on tasks or items that you can do, such as permissions for data collection, filing, and labelling materials for later use, researching and understanding the submission process for publications you want to target, socialising with family or friends, clearing and tidying your desk/workplace, updating your programme log and plan, reading articles, listening to podcasts relevant to your area of study, going for a run, walk, or swim. Planning and preparing meals to put into the deep freeze, researching conferences relevant to your study, submitting funding applications for conferences, and bursaries and so on, tidying and checking references and Digital Object Identifiers (DOI), drafting your thesis abstract, reading this book and trying out the activities which appeal to you, or to set up a "music to write/study playlist".

Potential tasks

The key to doctorate completion is to recognise that you are responsible for your progress. Academia often works at a different pace to mainstream environments, so, instead of waiting, focus on tasks that can be accomplished in the meantime. Review the list below and plan blocks of time to complete the tasks and align them with the deadlines and milestones of your institution.

1. Obtain permissions for data collection.
2. File and label folders and documents for easy reference.
3. Research and understand publication submission processes.
4. Socialise with family or friends.
5. Clear and tidy your workspace.
6. Update your program log and work plan.
7. Read articles or listen to podcasts relevant to the research.
8. Engage in physical activity such as running, walking, or swimming.
9. Plan and prepare meals for the deep freeze.
10. Research relevant conferences and meetings.
11. Submit funding applications.
12. Sort and verify references and check DOIs.
13. Draft the thesis abstract.
14. Read helpful books.
15. Try out unrelated activities that interest you.
16. Create a "music to write/study to" playlist (there is a TMSGTCAD one on YT Music and Spotify).
17. Seek ethical approval for your work.

Exercise: Filler tasks

Taking ownership of the process and remaining productive during slow periods increases the chance of completion. This 15- to 30-minute exercise, based on the Eisenhower Matrix, can help start the process (see Table 9.1). Develop a list of tasks that can be

completed during downtime on your research (see Table 9.2). They
are often framed as an I'll get around to this someday task, and can
include items such as: verifying references; data checks; contact,
information, and permission updates; text, data, and presentation
edits; setting appointments; recreation plans; update notes; conference research; review article, podcast or other material; training
module; check university research integrity code and so on.

TABLE 9.1 Filler task template

TASKS

DATE

Instructions:

1. Review your work plan.
2. List the "routine", "I'll get to this someday" tasks that you can
   complete in short bursts of time while waiting for feedback or have
   downtime on your work.
3. Consider items such as: verifying references, editing text, checking
   data, updating contacts, permissions, editing forms and presentations,
   virtual meetings, updating your notes, researching conferences,
   reading an article, research integrity checklist etc.
4. See Table 9.2: One Hundred Tasks while waiting for feedback for ideas.

IMPORTANT	URGENT

ROUTINE	I'LL GET TO THIS SOMEDAY

PRIORITY AREAS

1.
2.
3.

Filler Task Template. © 2023 Sinéad Hewson.

TABLE 9.2 One hundred tasks while waiting for feedback

15–30-minute tasks

✓ Adjust desk and chair height.
Check workspace lighting and
ventilation.

✓ Book chunks of time in the diary
to work on the doctorate. Book
days off!

✓ Check dates and paperwork for
annual review, transfer exam or
thesis defence.

✓ Check if there is an action to take
to get the answer you need to
move forward.

✓ Create a "music to write/study
to" playlist.

✓ Delegate – proactively delegate
tasks.

✓ Document specific requirements
for up-and-coming doctoral
committee meetings.

✓ Explore healthy food, meals, and
drink options.

✓ Fold the washing.

✓ Free write for 15 mins.

✓ Hydrate.

✓ Identify keywords.

✓ Join a peer group with other
candidates from the university
or sector.

✓ Logically label and file folders
and documents.

✓ Plan the week.

✓ Practise a new writing
technique.

✓ Register for relevant training/
seminars.

✓ Research and set up virtual
appointments with candidates
who have completed their
studies. Proactively seek advice.

✓ Set up and turn up at virtual
coffee appointments with
family, friends, and peers.

✓ Sort, check and verify a
reference and accompanying
DOI.

45–60-minute tasks

✓ Book dental and general health
check-ups.

✓ Brainstorm a title and tagline for
the thesis.

✓ Breathe.

✓ Clarify eligibility and apply for
study exemptions.

✓ Clean and tidy desk and
workspace.

✓ Complete a task from this (or a
similar) book.

✓ Confirm that registration for the
doctoral programme is complete.
Address any outstanding items.

✓ Create more storage space (on
and offline).

✓ Reach out to a peer, mentor, or
friend. Ask how they are and
how their work is progressing.

✓ Read articles, listen to podcasts,
watch videos relevant to the
research.

✓ Read part of this (or a similar)
book.

✓ Reflect and write on the
experience thus far. Are you in
or out of love with the
research? What needs to
change to thrive?

✓ Register on ORCID and
relevant academic/research
platforms.

(Continued)

TABLE 9.2 (Continued)

✓ Develop a list of 20 peers in the sector – find and follow relevant platforms, up-and-coming conferences, and publications.

✓ Develop a list of conferences and events worth attending.

✓ Do nothing.

✓ Draft a thank you note to those who helped with the study.

✓ Draft permission letter for research participants/to gain access to data.

✓ File research notes.

✓ Learn about logical fallacies.

✓ List and acknowledge programme achievements to date.

✓ Listen to a podcast and … iron, garden, walk.

✓ Look for logical fallacies in draft materials and before anything is submitted.

✓ Meditate.

✓ Plan physical, dental, health and mental wellbeing checks.

✓ Research and join relevant professional/academic groups that can aid progress.

✓ Research articles useful for the research.

✓ Research bursaries, funding applications, employment.

✓ Research target publications. What is the submission process?

✓ Review and document the university thesis structure requirements (format, page size, point size, headings, word count, structure, electronic or hard copy, etc.)

✓ Schedule and confirm progress meeting dates.

✓ Set up a folder/notebook to summarise key points from secondary research, such as articles and meetings relating to the research.

✓ Sort and delete emails and photos on devices.

✓ Sort apps and folders relating to the doctorate.

✓ Update deadlines and work plans.

✓ Visit international online libraries to search for specialist information on your topic.

✓ Watch a TED talk.

75-minute tasks

✓ Align the proposed work with university research integrity guidelines.

✓ Check DOI and document links.

✓ Check the data. Are there any errors or inconsistencies?

✓ Develop a privacy policy for the research.

✓ Develop an individual training and supervision plan for the programme. Update regularly.

✓ Plan the thesis layout. Focus on key points and mapping content.

✓ Prepare for the annual review.

✓ Read a selection of dissertations. Consider the quality of content, writing standard and readability.

✓ Read helpful books (like this one).

(Continued)

TABLE 9.2 (Continued)

✓ Discover good research practice resources. For example, the European Code of Research Integrity and university equivalent documents. Does your doctoral research comply? In what way specifically? Document note areas that need more work.

✓ Draft a mini presentation explaining the research.

✓ Draft a thesis checklist structured chapter by chapter. Include a list of forms/items that need to be included. Link ideas and concepts.

✓ Draft abstract text (aim for 300 to 500 words).

✓ Examine the current literature review. What would make it stronger?

✓ Explore and submit funding applications.

✓ Explore mindfulness activities such as meditation, yoga, painting, or deep breathing.

✓ Follow a series on a streaming service (and watch with friends).

✓ Go for a walk, swim, run or other form of exercise.

✓ Identify and review a useful article. Take notes.

✓ Meet family and friends for lunch.

✓ Meet friends.

✓ Meet the doctoral promoter/ sponsor for lunch.

✓ Network with other doctoral candidates.

✓ Network with peers.

✓ Obtain and document data collection permission.

✓ Pick and play a board game with family and friends.

✓ Plan and prepare deep-freeze meals.

✓ Plan and prepare nourishing meals.

✓ Research and draft budget costs for relevant conferences and events. Include the event name, valuable participant names, costs, potential to participate, and the benefits of attending).

✓ Research potential internal and external examiners for the transfer exam and thesis defence.

✓ Review and update the work plan.

✓ Review personal finances and establish a realistic budget. Brainstorm three ways to spend wisely.

✓ Review the project plan – what's going well? Is there something to catch up on?

✓ Review the university doctoral/ PhD handbook or checklist. List items for completion.

✓ Socialise with peers, family, and friends.

✓ Socialise: ring parents, friends, or siblings. Spend time with your partner, children, and friends. Have fun.

✓ Tidy and proofread citations.

✓ Tidy the data. Check for errors and inconsistencies.

✓ Try new activities that spark curiosity or are out of your comfort zone.

✓ Update logs with details of training, conferences, publications, etc.

✓ Update the program log provided by the university and review the work plan.

✓ Celebrate a milestone with friends and family. For example, progress to the next stage or a eureka moment.

One Hundred Tasks while waiting for feedback. © 2023 Sinéad Hewson.

Daily exercise: Reflection

Refer back to the exercises you have completed and ask daily:

1. What can I do to stay on track?
2. What do I need?
3. What steps will have the most impact for you to progress?
4. What is the difference that will make the difference to finish?

Weekly exercise: Words versus action

There are plans that you list … and there are plans that you carry out.

Ask:

1. Is there something I need to do this week?
2. What is it?
3. Make a concrete plan.
4. When is the best time to complete this (based on availability or how I work best)?
5. Where, when, and how will I do it?
6. Does it need to be broken into smaller steps?
7. Think about it, feel it, see it, smell it.
8. Experience it in vivid detail.

Exercise: Important versus urgent

The habit of categorising work into important, urgent, routine, I'll get to that someday helps on a weekly or monthly basis helps with the momentum of the doctoral thesis. Table 9.3 gives instructions on how to do this and the template (Table 9.4) can be adapted for your own use.

TABLE 9.3 Important versus urgent instructions

STEP 1:

1. Get a pen, some blank pages (A4 or larger), and post-its.
2. Write down ALL the things you must do on one or more pages.
3. Divide another page into four and allocate one heading to each panel. URGENT, IMPORTANT, PLANNED, and I'LL GET TO THIS SOMEDAY.
4. Review and edit the list of tasks into themes or chunks of activity on post-its.
5. Decide if the task is urgent, important, planned, or ad hoc.
6. Allocate the task under a specific heading.
7. Take a break, then review the list again.

STEP 2:

Review the tasks:

1. What do you want to achieve?
2. What's the purpose of your work?
3. What can you delegate?
4. What can you ignore or dump?
5. What one action will make a huge difference to your level of performance?

Note:
At first glance, the list may look chaotic. Review the actions and their purpose, and rewrite and chunk the list into smaller, more manageable pieces. When the to-do list flows, you automatically perform at a higher level.

STEP 3:

Rewrite the list, and allocate space in your diary for urgent, important, planned, and I'll get to it someday tasks.

Tip:
Set the completion date 2–3 days before the real due date to take the pressure off missed deadlines. For instance, Google Tasks is a simple way to capture tasks; it's free and easy to use.

STEP 4:

1. Review the work plan.
2. List the "routine" and "I'll get to this someday" tasks that can be completed in short bursts of time. Complete when waiting for feedback or have chunks of time available for small tasks.
3. Consider items such as: verifying references, editing text, checking data, updating contacts, permissions, editing forms and presentations, virtual meetings, updating your notes, researching conferences, reading an article, research integrity checklist etc.
4. See table: One Hundred Tasks while waiting for feedback for ideas.

One Hundred Tasks while waiting for feedback. © 2023 Sinéad Hewson.

TABLE 9.4 Important versus urgent template

TASKS

DATE

Instructions:
1. Fill in the template (see Table 9.3 for important versus urgent instructions)

IMPORTANT   **URGENT**

ROUTINE   **I'LL GET TO THIS SOMEDAY**

PRIORITY AREAS
   1.
   2.
   3.

Important versus urgent template. © 2023 Sinéad Hewson.

Monthly exercise: Reverse bucket list

Grab a cup of tea or water, a pen, and some paper and make a list. Think of items or habits that are not right for you now in your life. Then, focus on the doctoral work.

1. What items, tasks, or focus areas no longer serve me or the project?
2. Why?
3. Decide whether to delegate, defer, adapt, keep, or delete.
4. What are the consequences and benefits of this action?
5. Ask: Do I really need this?
6. Ask: Is this the best use of my time?
7. Take action.

Deadlines

"Learning to manage time. Learning to prioritise helped me."

PhD, Entrepreneurship

Fixed deadlines, for instance, for annual reviews, fall within an academic cycle, and if missed or an extension is requested, can run the risk of delaying progress to the next stage of a doctoral programme. Set an objective to meet critical deadlines and aim to complete early (rather than just on time). Check deadlines and progress against the plan and carefully prioritise the work.

There are situations when more time is needed: if this is the case, first of all, discuss and explain why with your supervisor or graduate research department and agree on a suitable course of action, as some deadlines are variable. An extension request requires formal approval, it is usually requested in writing and may require supporting evidence. Extensions are granted for personal or professional circumstances, to improve the quality of the work or gain access to specialist resources, services, or experts. In certain situations, it can be requested that doctoral studies be put on hold.

"There was a sudden illness in my family, and I became a full-time carer for a year. Although I was reading literature and scoping the research project, I did not submit a literature review or fulfil all requirements for the annual review. I spoke with my supervisor, who advised me to submit a letter explaining my circumstances and to supply original evidence of work completed, letters from my family member's medical specialist and GP confirming that I was caring, parenting, and self-employed and the impact of the family member's illness on my participation. My supervisor argued my case. The exam board granted permission to advance."

Part-time candidate, Communication

Journaling: awareness, self-reflection, and relevance

Most doctorate programmes require that candidates engage in a reflective process such as using a journal to facilitate awareness of and reflection on the candidates' preferences and presentation behaviour; to revisit and observe language choices in particular contexts and their effects; to consider the management of the project presentation of data and information; as a means to position the candidates' role as author in the final stages of the doctoral process.

The purpose of on-going evaluation is to establish an effective authorial identity and in turn script a strong argument for academic review (in the form of presentations, articles and ultimately the doctoral thesis). Over time, the thought process became clearer, and the maturation of concepts, research, findings, and conclusions are documented in annual assessments, presentations, and self-reflection exercises. Some candidates use mind maps and graphic facilitation images, others take copious notes, or they utilise templates to summarise key points within structured bullets and comments to capture concepts, ideas, and processes. This can aid the direction of the doctoral project and unpick complex ideas into bite-size, manageable pieces. It can help give form to primary research findings and organise the next step towards completion.

Getting things done

Committing to a long-term project like this means that there will be moments when you engage and disengage with the work. Setting writing targets, booking Focusmate sessions, or aiming to read an article and make brief notes are all examples of mini-targets that can help get the work done. The question is whether completing a task is the best use of your time at that moment. Sometimes, there are small chunks of time where you can ask – what can I complete with the time I have available?

INSIDER TIPS

Join the dots: Review the latest information – does it connect, add, or undermine what you have already?

To enhance creativity. Creativity is not only a matter of sudden inspiration. Connecting the dots generates new concepts and approaches.

Check references, citations, and DOIs: Use downtime to verify that references, links, and DOIs are accurate and that the links work.

Note: A DOI is a string of numbers, letters, and symbols that uniquely identify an article or document and provide it with a permanent web address (URL). Cite articles with DOIs that are credible easy to find and manually check that the links work.

▶ SUMMARY

The focus of this chapter was on finishing, and a series of daily, monthly, and weekly exercises and questions were presented to help understand preferred ways of working, identify priorities, and build a realistic work routine of work, planning schedule, and ways to track results.

Key terms

Important versus urgent
One hundred tasks while waiting for feedback
Staying on track

> "I have a wall chart in my home office. I can see where I am in the process, how many words I have written."
>
> Part-time PhD, History

▶ USEFUL RESOURCES AND REFERENCES

References

Clear, J. (2018). *Atomic habits* (p. 27). London: Random House. Kindle Edition: ISBN: 9781473537804.

Covey, S. R. (2004). *The 7 habits of highly effective people: Restoring the character ethic.* New York: Free Press: ISBN: 9780743272452, 9780743269513, 9781417656646, 0743272455, 0743269519, 1417656646.

Dweck, C. S. (2017). *Mindset - Updated edition: Changing the way you think to fulfil your potential* (p. 260). London: Little, Brown Book Group: Kindle Edition: ISBN: 978-1-47213-996-2.

Kouzes, J. M., & Posner, B. Z. (2018). *The student leadership challenge: Five practices for becoming an exemplary leader.* San Francisco: Wiley. Kindle Edition: ISBN: 978-1-119-42191-7, 978-1-119-42224-2, 978-1-119-42225-9.

Mantai, L. (2019). 'A source of sanity': The role of social support for doctoral candidates' belonging and becoming. *International Journal of Doctoral Studies, 14,* 367–382. doi:https://doi.org/10.28945/4275

Thomas, D. (2016). *The PhD writing handbook* (pp. 175, 177–184). London: Palgrave Macmillan: ISBN 978-1-137-49769-7.

Resources

Five Practises of Exemplary Leadership. https://www.leadershipchallenge.com/research/five-practices.aspx

TMSGTCAD Playlist on YT Music. https://music.youtube.com/playlist?list=PLzUK2DUSaody5RGNW_iY-C6gHmnfQwcSa

10 Feedback and setbacks

> "I had two supervisors who actively supported my research. Their role was to test, unpick and challenge the content I created so that the body of work produced at the end of the research journey was robust and 'bulletproof'. It was bruising."
>
> Mature PhD, Recognition of Prior Learning.

▶ INTRODUCTION

Understanding the purpose and value of feedback – even when it is harsh is a critical part of the doctoral process. For mature students who already hold leadership positions in their area of expertise, critical feedback is hard to hear or appears to undermine what you bring to the table or is simply not helpful. Feedback in all forms is a means to strengthen or affirm your point of view. It creates an opportunity to consider alternatives you had not considered before. It is a means to gather these insights, process them, and construct new knowledge.

When feedback is honest and critical and acts as a stimulus to produce better work, it is helpful and clear, and the individual will

DOI: 10.4324/9781003413691-13

say something like, "I will learn much from it, even if someone is difficult". This aspect of deep learning helps ensure good outcomes. That is the focus of this chapter.

Types of feedback

There are three types of feedback that doctoral candidates, in general, receive. Accept, which means minimal or no changes. Adapt where the candidate is requested to revise the work, make changes, learn from the feedback, and resubmit. Abandon, which means to stop, learn from the rejection, and reconsider next steps inside or outside of academia.

Feedback is directed at your research, not you. Therefore, respond (don't react). Ask for clarification. Discuss with peers. Share your paper and get feedback. Be realistic, for instance, in the case of annual reviews, journal, and thesis submissions, feedback with recommendations to adapt is common (Dweck, 2017; Thomas, 2016; Gosling and Noordam, 2011).

INSIGHT

"Practise patience. I was asked to make changes in the final stages of my thesis. I did not agree with all of the points and was advised to include them so that the work would progress to the viva stage. Although I passed the oral defence, both examiners requested minor edits, and the final version of the document pretty much reverted back to the earlier draft."

Part-time PhD by research

There is a choice when receiving feedback – you can accept it, reflect on it, or reject it. When you examine the comments, in most cases, the reviewer is asking you to reframe an argument so that it is clearer, understandable, or more robust. Even when you disagree with the points made, thank the individual, reflect as to whether it is relevant or not to the work, and then decide what action you will take.

How you behave when handling feedback links back to the *motivation* behind the doctorate. When you are clear on your outcome, you have a choice in how you behave in certain situations and can take responsibility for the work. It also enables you to be adaptable and control your state (how you react to situations). When the opposite is the case – not knowing what you want – there is a risk of being at the mercy of your own emotions, being judgemental, or blaming others when things don't go your way. There is a clear distinction between knowing why you want to do something and having an unwavering emotional connection to get it done. That is why a substantial project, like a PhD, needs a powerful why.

INSIDER TIP

Consider feedback as an opportunity to strengthen your body of work. Ask: will it generate useful information or more of the same? Then, review and reframe the feedback a few times. Understand what the person is really saying.

Exercise: Feedback framework

Create a list/table, categorise the feedback, document the actions you need to take (by when), and track progress: adopting a Growth Mindset can help generate new choices and alternative courses of action to help with feedback (see Table 10.1).

For instance, feedback on writing styles can be confused, misdirected, agree, disagree, or be contradictory. The most effective manner to receive feedback is to give thanks, reflect on their points, and decide whether to take on board some, all, or none of what they say.

TABLE 10.1 Exercise: Feedback framework

Feedback framework

STEP 1: When reviewing feedback, reflect:

1. This is helpful! – it improves the work. I will address this by …
2. I don't understand this point. What is the reviewer trying to say? Do I need to seek clarification on this point?
3. The reviewer did not understand my point, did they not understand or misread my work? Do I need to make this point more clearly next time?
4. Poorly articulated point. What needs to change to make this point more clearly?
5. Contradictions. They said this here and contradicted themselves there. I said this here and contradicted myself there.
6. I agree with this point (explain).
7. I disagree with this point (explain).
8. This is based on my/or the journal's writing style.
9. Did the feedback say anything about my individuality?

STEP 2: Circulate for supervisor feedback or peer review.

Feedback framework © 2023 Sinéad Hewson.

▶ **WHEN YOU GET STUCK**

The one-to-one interview participants said that we all get stuck at different stages of the doctoral process and their advice is summarised in Table 10.2 Ten tips for when you get stuck.

INSIGHT

"I included a number of recommendations from my supervisor that I did not fully agree with and did so, so that I could progress and pass the transfer exam. I realised it was better to use my time to focus on the bigger picture rather than nitpick on small things that had no impact on the research. Mind you, it took a lot of to-ing and fro-ing for me to recognise this."

Part-time PhD, Communication

Take a break – go for a walk if you are getting frustrated. Re-read the feedback with a constructive frame of mind. Ask what needs to change for me to get through this phase? What actions do I need to take to move this forward? Work on the hardest thing first and chunk it into manageable actions. Focus on the major changes (in case you have to make a significant change to something or revisit an area). The smaller, quicker changes can be inserted at a later stage in small chunks of time.

Ten tips for when you get stuck

TABLE 10.2 Ten tips for when you get stuck

1. When the voice in your head says "I'm not an academic, a writer, a scientist, an artist", act as if and reframe your words: "I am a writer, a subject matter expert, an authority on …"

2. Finished is better than perfect. Get the idea and points you want to make on paper … perfection comes later. Work one step at a time?

3. Record your points out loud (out walking, in the car (if it is safe to do so), in front of the mirror, send a voice message to yourself then and get it on paper). Let the ideas flow.

4. Move items on the page – consider testing writing tools like Scrivener and play with the layout of the text. Keep backups of old versions of documents. Free-write and use writing prompts to hone your ideas.

5. Cull your sentences and condense the points you want to make into a tight, coherent sentence, phrase, or keywords.

6. Establish a writing routine – close the door when you are not writing. Sometimes, small kids are like magnets – keep them occupied with fun things while you write. Are you an early bird or a night owl? Me. I'm an afternoon person:)

7. Remove distractions – go offline (Freedom app, Focusmate, Scrivener).

8. Start and develop different parts of the thesis – you don't have to start at the beginning – build a foundation, develop key points, build and grow content.

9. Follow a template – adapt to meet your study needs.

10. Set personal deadlines (they act as a map – not a stick to beat yourself up with).

Ten tips for when you get stuck. © 2023 Sinéad Hewson.

▶ SETBACKS

"My supervisor pretty much said the structure of my draft thesis sucked even though I followed the rubric provided by the university. He said I had to work out what was wrong myself. I was willing to accept most of the points he raised. Some of the feedback contradicted what I had experienced in the industry I work in. I took a break, nursed my bruised ego and then brainstormed ways restructuring could strengthen the body of work."

Part-time PhD, Communication

Dweck's advice when you hit a setback is to let it do its thing. When things settle, reflect, have a conversation with yourself, ask how you plan to learn from the setback (Dweck, 2017). Identify ways the setback can be used to make the doctoral work even better (Gosling and Noordam, 2011). Look at the issue from the viewpoint of your perspective, that of your supervisor/ examiner, a peer critiquing the work, and a neutral observer. This approach pushes emotion aside, and if you were to ask the advice of a neutral observer or confidant: What do they see? What would they say? What, in their words, is the message behind the setback?

It is normal to vent when the unexpected happens. Whenever you experience a sense of rejection or pressure, acknowledge it, take a breath, and then work out what to do next. Secret worries about confirming a stereotype (Dweck 2017) or feeling the burden of representation can occur if you are in a Fixed Mindset. If you notice you are moving towards overwhelm, talk to a trusted confidant and seek support. When you are in a Growth Mindset, the stereotype does not disrupt performance. In fact, it makes people better able to defend their point of view and thrive.

Exercise: Plans change

Chapter 3 opens with a message to stick to deadlines. However, circumstances change, and once you have developed a plan, it needs regular updates and will look very different as the doctoral project progresses. When you have updated your plan, ask: When, where, and how I will act on my new plan? Have a conversation with your Fixed Mindset persona to tell you ways it won't work and to offer reasonable alternatives to bring it to fruition and turn it into a better plan. Notice what comes up.

INSIDER TIP

The power of YET. When you get stuck or don't know what to do next. Tell yourself I don't know how to complete that yet and work out what you can do to move forward or build a skill.

Errors

We all make mistakes. Errors can occur in our work, and in most cases, they are honest errors. In academia, an honest error requires the publication of a correction when detected. Corrections are also necessary for factual errors. Pervasive errors can result from a coding problem or a miscalculation and can result in extensive inaccuracies throughout an article to dissertation. If this type of error does not change the direction or significance of the results, interpretations, and conclusions of the article or thesis, then a correction should be published. However, errors that are serious enough to invalidate a paper's results and thesis conclusions may require retraction or withdrawal from a publication or doctoral process.

▶ SUMMARY

Strategies for handling feedback and setbacks were briefly covered in this chapter and expanded further in *Part IV: Wellbeing.*

The point is, when you receive unexpected feedback, there are four choices. Accept it, reject it, adapt it, or defend it. Stay curious, not furious. Let it go, then move on.

Key terms

Feedback
Fixed and Growth Mindsets
Setbacks

> Use feedback and setbacks as a way to strengthen you and the work. Take care of yourself.

▶ USEFUL RESOURCES AND REFERENCES

References

Covey, S. R. (2004). *The 7 habits of highly effective people: Restoring the character ethic.* New York: Free Press: ISBN: 9780743272452, 9780743269513, 9781417656646, 0743272455, 0743269519, 1417656646.

Dweck, C. S. (2017). *Mindset - Updated edition: Changing the way you think to fulfil your potential* (p. 260). London: Little, Brown Book Group: Kindle Edition: ISBN: 978-1-47213-996-2.

Gosling, P., & Noordam, L. D. (2011). *Mastering your PhD; Survival and success in the doctoral years and beyond.* Berlin: Springer: 978-3-642-15847-6, doi: 10.1007/978-3-642-15847-6.

Thomas, D. (2016). *The PhD writing handbook* (pp. 175, 177–184). London: Palgrave Macmillan: ISBN: 978-1-137-49769-7.

The viva

▶ INTRODUCTION

The viva or thesis defence is the highlight of the doctoral process. It is the one time when you have the opportunity to talk in-depth about the research with peers who have read the material and have prepared a series of questions, comments, and feedback to confirm that the entire body of work is worthy of a doctoral award.

The introductory chapter discussed programme learning goals and doctoral learning outcomes (Table 1.1) and went on to say that a doctorate is awarded to students who demonstrate a systematic understanding of a field of study and mastery of the skills and research methods in that field. They act as a reference point to revisit and document the expected and unexpected experiences of the programme (Table 11.1 Have I fulfilled the requirements to be awarded a doctoral degree?)

▶ PREPARING FOR THE VIVA

When preparing for the viva, focus on the positive aspects of the doctoral experience. What did you gain? How did you grow? The PhD is an investment in you and your ideas, and possibly the only

DOI: 10.4324/9781003413691-14

Table 11.1 Have I fulfilled the requirements to be awarded a doctoral degree?

1. KNOWLEDGE AND UNDERSTANDING

  1.2 Broad knowledge and understanding of my research field/subject matter area.
Point 1:
Point 2:
Point 3:

  1.3 In-depth, up-to-date specialist knowledge and state-of-the-art in a particular area.
Point 1:
Point 2:
Point 3:

2. PROFICIENCY AND ABILITY

  2.1 Critically analyse, examine, and review facts, issues, and situations
Point 1:
Point 2:
Point 3:

  2.2 Operate with intellectual independence. Act ethically and with integrity
Point 1:
Point 2:
Point 3:

  2.3 Identify and formulate research questions critically, objectively, and creatively.
Point 1:
Point 2:
Point 3:

  2.4 Design, plan, and conduct research adopting appropriate methods with scientific rigour.
Point 1:
Point 2:
Point 3:

  2.5 Complete tasks and reach milestones in a timely manner.
Point 1:
Point 2:
Point 3:

  2.6 Review and evaluate the work and articulate the findings.
Point 1:
Point 2:
Point 3:

TABLE 11.1 (Continued)

2.7 A significant contribution to the development of knowledge by completing a substantial project and (depending on the type of doctorate) writing a thesis and/or several academic articles or commentary of prior publication/portfolio.
Point 1:
Point 2:
Point 3:

2.8 Communicate by presenting and discussing the research, results, and the case for examination orally and in writing amongst peers and the general public nationally and internationally.
Point 1:
Point 2:
Point 3:

2.9 Present work logically and coherently following international codes of practice.
Point 1:
Point 2:
Point 3:

2.10 Contribute to society and support the learning of others.
Point 1:
Point 2:
Point 3:

3. JUDGEMENT AND APPROACH

3.1 Act with intellectual independence, (research) integrity.
Point 1:
Point 2:
Point 3:

3.2 The ability to make ethical decisions and judgements.
Point 1:
Point 2:
Point 3:

3.3 Personal accountability.
Point 1:
Point 2:

Content adapted from multiple sources, including:

European Code for Research Integrity 2017 and 2023; Karolinska Institutet 2023; National Framework for Doctoral Education, HEA 2017; Articulating learning outcomes in doctoral education. Washington, DC: Council of Graduate Schools 2017; The PhD Viva, P. Smith 2014; European Higher Education Area & Bologna Process 2005; The Higher Education Ordinance, Annexe 2, Sweden, 1993.

IMPORTANT: This self-reflection framework is for illustration purposes only. Universities may have additional requirements and highlight specific skill sets necessary to meet award criteria.

Have I fulfilled the requirements to be awarded a Doctoral Degree? © 2023 Sinéad Hewson.

time in your life when you can delve deep into a subject because you want to or because you have something to say on a particular issue. Treat the viva as a transformational experience, be mindful of published information focused on survival and being reduced to tears. Some frame it as a fearful experience, something to be afraid of, when it is not (Smith, 2014; Thomas, 2016). At the viva you share your expertise and work with peers, present, discuss, and demonstrate how it contributes to new knowledge. The examiner's role is to validate, ask robust questions, and agree on an outcome.

INSIGHTS

"I'm doing it for me because I genuinely have something to say."

Part-time PhD, Communication

"It is a privilege to do this."

Part-time PhD, History

INSIDER TIP

Connect with like-minded peers.

The following pages contain a number of templates to help you prepare. First of all, you will review your dissertation, publication, and work using the doctoral learning outcomes as a guide. Ask:

Good viva/thesis defence preparation

Start preparing a couple of weeks before the defence. First of all, check that the date is confirmed and that all the necessary paperwork has been submitted. Then, read through the thesis and reflect on why you loved working on it and its importance. Examine every page – identify the most important message on each one, list potential questions. If there are any typos or errors, document them noting the page, paragraph, and link and how to correct it (Smith, 2014).

Although the examiners have read your work in advance of the defence, you will be required to present key points and point out areas of specific interest to your peers. This can be a challenge for candidates – how can you condense four to seven years of work into a 20- or 30-minute presentation? Check the guidelines for your faculty and start preparations early.

Organise a mock viva with the supervisor to run through the defence presentation. Encourage them to ask awkward questions. Seek feedback to improve the presentation and refine the answers (Dweck, 2017). "Scrape the internet." Ask AI for potential questions. Develop a master list of potential questions and answers. Prepare answers in bullet point format.

Rehearse the presentation, arrive early to the location and enjoy. Vivas are like a meeting of minds. You are there to tell the story of the research, your own doctoral journey, and answer questions. The role of the examiner is to ensure that you know what you are talking about, that it is your own work, and to understand why you made the choices that you made and to get a sense of your contribution to scholarly discussion.

It is a formal process, embrace it.

Transfer exam/viva checklist

I have:

1. Re-read the thesis (and/or the transfer exam submission document).
2. Drafted a one-page summary for each chapter.
3. Summarised each page in one or two bullet points.
4. Completed a mock viva with my supervisor.

5. Kept a list of errors/minor amendments to make after the viva.
6. Drafted a list of potential questions.
7. Prepared a presentation for the meeting.
8. Highlighted areas/key points I want to cover at the session and why.
9. Developed flash cards linking key ideas and references.
10. Confirmed the location, time, and date of the meeting and know how to get there.
11. Kept up to date with the literature.
12. Indicated to examiners the proposed next steps in my presentation/questions (for example an article, product development etc.).
13. Spoken to peers for feedback and tips.
14. Clarified the technical setup and checked that my presentation is compatible.
15. Explained key points from the work in plain language.
16. Re-read the viva/defence guidelines for my institution.
17. The necessary paperwork completed.
18. Practised my presentation several times and checked it is within acceptable time limits.
19. Organised a mock viva with my supervisor.
20. Ensured that I understand the process, the outcome, when I will be informed, and the next steps.
21. Scheduled a block of time to complete any edits proposed by the examiners, followed by time off.

INSIDER TIP

Reviewing Data and Text. Go through every page of data and text. Ask: In what way does this text/data add value to the body of work? What is the point I am trying to make? Should this content be included, adapted, or deleted? Is it nice to include or essential to include? What is the reason for this choice?

▶ PREPARING THE PRESENTATION

You cannot include everything in your presentation. The following tables follow the same structure as the thesis format from Chapter 6. It will help you determine what should be included in the viva voce presentation (see Tables 11.2 through to 11.10, and also 11.12). The structure should be logical, coherent, and easy to follow. It should contain key information for use in the defence (Smith, 2014; Bloomberg, 2023).

TABLE 11.2 Viva voce: Slide 1: Title page

Date:	Version:

Purpose:

1. Clearly and concisely describe the research topic or problem.
2. Identify the author(s) as the owner(s) of the work.

IT SHOULD CONTAIN	ASK
Slide 1: Title page: (follow university guidelines)	1. Does the title clearly convey what the presentation is about?
○ Title.	2. Is it understandable?
○ Author's full name.	3. Use the notes function to remember the page numbers of key points in the thesis.
○ The degree to be conferred.	
○ University, department & college.	
○ Date	

Format: (follow university guidelines)

PRIORITY AREAS

1.
2.
3.

WHAT MAKES THIS SLIDE EXCELLENT?

1.
2.
3.

Viva Voce: Slide 1: Title Page. © 2023 Sinéad Hewson.

TABLE 11.3 Viva voce: Slide 2: Agenda/introduction

Date: *Version:*

Purpose:

1. Organise and present content in a logical order.
2. Provide a detailed overview of the presentation.
3. Acts as a signpost for the examiners and moderators to navigate the work.
4. Introduce the thesis and the research problem.
5. Set the scene for the presentation (the importance of the topic, the gap in knowledge, the purpose, and value of the study).

IT SHOULD CONTAIN

Slide 2: Agenda/introduction: (follow university guidelines)

o Introduction
o Research focus
o Motivation
o Literature review
o Methodology
o Study Overview
o Results
o Conclusions
o Contribution
o Questions & close

Format: (follow university guidelines)

CHECK THAT

1. Headings and subheadings accurately reflect the material contained in the main body of the presentation.
2. The layout and format comply with the awarding institution's guidelines.
3. The headings and subheadings are grammatically consistent (language, spelling, tone and tense).
4. Use the notes function to remember the page numbers of key points in the thesis.

PRIORITY AREAS

1.
2.
3.

WHAT MAKES THIS SLIDE EXCELLENT?

1.
2.
3.

TABLE 11.4 Viva voce:
Slide 3: Research focus

Date: *Version:*

Purpose:

1. Introduces the research problem/question.
2. It is understandable, informative, and precise.

IT SHOULD CONTAIN   **CHECK THAT**

Slide 3: Research focus

○ The research problem/question

Format: (follow university guidelines)

1. It sets the scene for the study.
2. Language is informative, concise, and accurate.
3. There are no typos.
4. Use the notes function to remember the page numbers of key points in the thesis.

PRIORITY AREAS

1.
2.
3.

WHAT MAKES THIS SLIDE EXCELLENT?

1.
2.
3.

Viva Voce: Slide 3: Research focus. © 2023 Sinéad Hewson.

TABLE 11.5 Viva voce: Slide 4: Motivation

Date:	Version:

Purpose:

1. Why is the study needed?
2. Justify in terms of the literature.
3. Background to my work.
4. Ask: Why did you undertake this study?
5. Ask: How can you justify it?
6. Ask about the purpose of the research and the reason I wanted to work on it.

IT SHOULD CONTAIN

Slide 4: Motivation

○ Why is the study needed?
○ Justify in terms of the literature.
○ Justify in terms of my background and experience.

Graphics/images:

○ Experience
○ Academic discourse
○ Build knowledge
○ Curiosity

CHECK THAT

1. Content is relevant and relates to the problem statement, the purpose of the study, and the research question/hypothesis.
2. Is factual, accurate, and concise.
3. Use the notes function to remember the page numbers of key points in the thesis.

PRIORITY AREAS

1.
2.
3.

WHAT MAKES THIS SLIDE EXCELLENT?

1.
2.
3.

Viva Voce: Slide 4: Motivation. © 2023 Sinéad Hewson.

TABLE 11.6 Viva voce: Slide 5: Literature review

Date:	Version:

Purpose:

1. Provide an overview of current scholarly knowledge (theories, models, and concepts).
2. Identify where the study sits within the academic/sectoral landscape.
3. Identify gaps or problems with the current knowledge and ways a study can address that gap.
4. Provide a theoretical or conceptual framework of the study to guide the research, analysis, and synthesis of the findings later in the process.
5. How does the literature underpin my work?

IT SHOULD CONTAIN

Slide 5: Literature review

o Overview of relevant literature
o Key authors and papers
o Explain why the study is needed
o What is the gap in the literature
o How does the literature underpin my work?

CHECK THAT

1. Content is relevant and relates to the problem statement, the purpose of the study and the research question/hypothesis.
2. Includes a diagram mapping the key factors to aid understanding.
3. Is factual, accurate, and concise.
4. Use the notes function to remember the page numbers of key points in the thesis.

PRIORITY AREAS

1.
2.
3.

WHAT MAKES THIS SLIDE EXCELLENT?

1.
2.
3.

Viva voce: Slide 5: Literature review. ©2023 Sinéad Hewson.

TABLE 11.7 Viva voce: Slide 6: Methodology

Date:	Version:

Purpose:

1. It describes the methodology (the approach) used to address the research question/hypothesis.
2. It justifies the rationale and reasoning for that approach.
3. It describes the research context, sample, and inclusion criteria.
4. Clearly describes data collection and analysis methods.
5. Details the study design, procedures, and policies.
6. Demonstrate knowledge of research theory of the PhD candidate/author(s).

IT SHOULD CONTAIN

Slide 6:
Methodology

○ Explain my methodological approach.
○ Why did I choose this approach over others?
○ Present the methods used in the study.
○ Mention any ethical issues.
○ Highlight the limitations of my approach.

CHECK THAT

1. Content is coherent and well-organised.
2. The methodology is clearly explained and properly justified.
3. That the approach makes the study replicable (FAIR principles).
4. Uses where possible diagrams, figures and tables to illustrate an important point (Dey, 1993).
5. Use the notes function to remember the page numbers of key points in the thesis.

PRIORITY AREAS

1.
2.
3.

WHAT MAKES THIS SLIDE EXCELLENT?

1.
2.
3.

Viva Voce: Slide 6: Methodology. © 2023 Sinéad Hewson.

TABLE 11.8 Viva voce: Slide 7: Results

Date:	Version:

Purpose:

1. Organise and objectively report the study's main findings in detail.
2. It acts as the foundation for the analysis, conclusions, and recommendations chapters of the thesis.

IT SHOULD CONTAIN

Slide 7: Results

○ Present the main results.
○ Discuss what they mean.
○ Relate them to the literature.
○ How did I evaluate my work?
○ How does it compare with others in the field?

CHECK THAT

1. The material contains enough detail to tell the story of the research findings.
2. The introduction reminds the reader of the purpose of the study.
3. The content is coherent and well-organised.
4. Uses where possible diagrams, figures, and tables to illustrate an important point.
5. Findings are clear, trustworthy, transparent, and objective.
6. Findings are presented following the format of the research question or hypothesis and/or themes identified through primary and secondary research.
7. Unexpected results are addressed appropriately.

PRIORITY AREAS

1.
2.
3.

WHAT MAKES THIS SLIDE EXCELLENT?

1.
2.
3.

Viva Voce: Slide 7: Results. © 2023 Sinéad Hewson.

TABLE 11.9 Viva voce: Slide 8: AI/automated

Date:	Version:

Purpose:

1. Declare the use of AI/automation.
2. Discuss the impact of AI/automation on the research (benefits and limitations).

IT SHOULD CONTAIN	CHECK THAT
Slide 8: AI/automated ○ Elements in the submitted thesis which were automated. ○ Elements of the study which used AI.	1. Did automation have a positive effect on a. actual quality of the final product? b. perceived quality of the final product? 2. Introduce discussion points on custom-built code for the sector to identify areas of disruption. 3. Highlight the areas of disruption (syntax, incorrect automated references etc.).

PRIORITY AREAS

1.
2.
3.

WHAT MAKES THIS SLIDE EXCELLENT?

1.
2.
3.

Viva Voce: Slide 8: AI/automated. © 2023 Sinéad Hewson.

TABLE 11.10 Viva voce: Slide 9: Conclusions

Date:	*Version:*

Purpose:

1. Demonstrate the significance of the study.
2. Summarise the research findings and their meaning (concluding statements).
3. Discuss the implications of the findings and link back to issues raised in earlier chapters and the literature.
4. Consider the significance of the study in the sector and within the wider academic community.
5. Discuss the limitations of the study and recommendations for further examination and/or continuity of the research.

IT SHOULD CONTAIN	CHECK THAT
Slide 9: Conclusions ○ Conclusions and recommendations ○ Implications in academia, the sector, in the wider community.	1. It sums up the research findings and includes a set of recommendations and next steps for the sector. 2. It refers to and builds on points raised in earlier chapters. 3. The conclusions are accurate and reflect the insights drawn from the research findings and analysis. 4. The content is credible, coherent, and well-organised. 5. The arguments are well thought through, trustworthy, transparent, and objective. 6. Ask: Have I answered the research question? 7. Ask: Does the chapter reflect the quality of the work? Is it credible? 8. Ask: Does the presentation structure follow the reporting guidelines of my discipline? 9. Ask: Does it help the audience gain an understanding of the new knowledge which emerged from the study? 10. Reflect: In what ways does the entire body of work position me as an expert?

PRIORITY AREAS

1.
2.
3.

WHAT MAKES THIS SLIDE EXCELLENT?

1.
2.
3.

Viva Voce: Slide 9: Conclusions. © 2023 Sinéad Hewson.

TABLE 11.11 Viva voce: Slide 10: Contribution

Date: *Version:*

Purpose:

1. Discuss contribution to knowledge.
2. Contribution I am most proud of.

IT SHOULD CONTAIN

Slide 10: Contribution

○ Contribution to knowledge
○ What I am most proud of

CHECK THAT

1. Reflect: In what ways does the entire body of work position me as an expert?

PRIORITY AREAS

1.
2.
3.

WHAT MAKES THIS SLIDE EXCELLENT?

1.
2.
3.

Viva Voce: Slide 10: Contribution. © 2023 Sinéad Hewson.

TABLE 11.12 Viva voce: Slide 11: Questions and close

Date:	Version:

Purpose:

1. Conclude the presentation
2. Key message/takeaway from the work
3. Acknowledgement and thanks
4. Answer questions

IT SHOULD CONTAIN

Slide 11: Questions and close

○ Take away message
○ Thanks
○ Close
○ Q&A

CHECK THAT

1. The presentation stays within the set time.
2. Mock questions are answered in advance of the session.
3. I can answer the question I hope they don't ask?

PRIORITY AREAS

1.
2.
3.

WHAT MAKES THIS SLIDE EXCELLENT?

1.
2.
3.

Viva Voce: Slide 11: Questions and close. © 2023 Sinéad Hewson.

What will they ask?

Examiners are there to clarify that the research is your own, original work, that you understand what you did, and that your work and expertise are worthy of a PhD. They want to know what you did, why you did it, and how it relates to other work? Is it publishable? Did you achieve what you set out to achieve? How did you do that (i.e., prove your hypothesis)? What are the implications of your findings?

▶ SUMMARY

This chapter focused on the viva, preparing and reminding you why you have invested time and effort to grow your expertise and develop new knowledge. When you have received the result of the viva voce it will either be resubmit, award with major edits, award with minor edits, award with no edits. The majority of candidates are requested to edit their thesis. Consider this a normal part of the process and allocate adequate time to complete the work.

I wish you well in your viva exam. You've got this.

Key terms

Doctoral learning outcomes
Generic viva voce presentation
Page by page thesis review
Preparation
Viva voce

> "Love your PhD and it will love you."
>
> Part-time PhD, Theology.

▶ USEFUL RESOURCES AND REFERENCES

References

ALLEA. (2023). *The European Code of Conduct for research integrity – Revised Edition 2023*. Berlin. doi:10.26356/ECOC; ISBN: 978-3-9823562-3-5.

Bloomberg, L.D. (2023). *Completing your qualitative dissertation: A road map from beginning to end*. London: SAGE Publications. Kindle Edition: ISBN: 978-1-0718-6981-9.

Bloomberg, L. D., and Volpe, M. (2008). *Completing your qualitative dissertation: A roadmap from beginning to end. Part 1: Taking charge of yourself and your work*. Sage Publications. doi:10.4135/9781452226613.

Borrell-Damian, L. (2009). *Collaborative Doctoral Education. University-industry partnerships for enhancing knowledge exchange. DOC-CAREERS Project*. Brussels: EUA: ISBN: 9789078997139.

Denecke, D., Kent, J., & McCarthy, M. T. (2017). *Articulating learning outcomes in doctoral education*. Washington, DC: Council of Graduate Schools. ISBN: 10-digit 1-933042-51-6, 13-digit 978-1-933042-51-0.

Dey, I. (1993). *Qualitative data analysis: A user-friendly guide for social scientists* (pp. 85, 103, 201, 250). New York: Routledge: ISBN: 9780203412497.

Dweck, C. S. (2017). *Mindset - Updated edition: Changing the way you think to fulfil your potential*. London: Little, Brown Book Group: Kindle Edition: ISBN: 978-1-47213-996-2.

European Higher Education Area. (2005). https://www.ehea.info/media. ehea.info/file/WG_Frameworks_qualification/85/2/Framework_ qualificationsforEHEA-May2005_587852.pdf

HEA. (2017). *National Framework for Doctoral Education*. https://hea. ie/assets/uploads/2017/04/national_framework_for_doctoral_ education_0.pdf

Mantai, L. (2019). 'A source of sanity': The role of social support for doctoral candidates' belonging and becoming. *International Journal of Doctoral Studies, 14*, 367–382. https://doi.org/10.28945/4275

Smith, P. (2014). *The PhD viva* (1st ed.). London: Bloomsbury Publishing. ISBN: 9781137395764.

The Higher Education Ordinance (1993). *Annexe 2*, Sweden.

Thomas, D. (2016). *The PhD writing handbook* (pp. 175, 177–184). London: Palgrave Macmillan: ISBN: 978-1-137-49769-7.

Resources

Broad A. Nasty PhD Viva Questions, University of Calgary. https://pages.
    cpsc.ucalgary.ca/~saul/wiki/uploads/Chapter1/NastyPhDQuestions.
    html
The Guardian. (2015). *How to survive a PhD Viva.* https://www.the
    guardian.com/higher-education-network/2015/jan/08/how-to-survive-
    a-phd-viva-17-top-tips
The Page Doctor. (2021). *How to prepare for the PhD Viva in 10 days.*
    https://www.thepagedoctor.com/how-to-prepare-for-the-phd-
    viva-in-10-days/
Vitae. (2023). *Thesis defence checklist.* https://www.vitae.ac.uk/doing-
    research/doing-a-doctorate/completing-your-doctorate/your-viva/
    viva-checklist

Part IV
Wellbeing

Focus on self

INSIGHTS

"We all have a perfect pace that we work at. When you are in the flow, hit the stride, you can run forever. We are all different. When we are in the flow – the key is pacing yourself so that you don't burn out."

Novelist, former PhD proofreader

"I think one of the challenges, which is more personal, is that it is a lonely journey. if you're not self-motivated, you can easily give up."

PhD, Theology

▶ INTRODUCTION

When part-time and mature candidates turn up and are accepted onto programmes, they bring industry knowledge, know-how, and life experience to the table. The doctorate is more than an award at the highest level. For them, it is a transformation programme which requires deep thinking and commitment. The journey towards completion is a marathon; milestones act as markers and signposts, and completion is a major life achievement.

DOI: 10.4324/9781003413691-16

Scholarly articles on doctoral completion tend to adopt process loss language patterns framed in negatively visual, fault-based terms rather than beneficial, outcome-orientated gains. For example, the difficulties of balancing wellbeing, academic endeavour and productivity using descriptors such as hardship, challenges, stress, survival, pain, or uncertainty. Although part-time, mature, and under-represented groups have a higher risk of dropping out, they are an invisible cohort within the literature and in terms of institutional support, customised resources, and recognition. The experiences of candidates who don't fit the standard profile in the literature are documented from an academic perspective rather than through the lens of a "perpetual outsider" going through the process (Archer, 2008; Gardner and Holley, 2011; Shavers and Moore, 2019).

The Wheel of Life® framework (Figure 2.2), which was used in the Maintaining a Sense of Balance exercise (Table 2.2), is used again to explore *wellbeing*, the fourth doctoral completion trigger, because the ability to own your doctorate and act with purpose, clarity, and intent depends on looking out for yourself and knowing where to focus your efforts.

Understanding why you feel the way you do

A PhD aims to develop independent researchers (Neumann and Tan, 2011), and the type of supportive environment impacts the performance, progression, and wellbeing of candidates (Peltonen et al., 2017). PhDs who do not fit the standard profile and part-time candidates need to be recognised and understood and their needs met to create a sense of belonging in academia (Shavers and Moore 2014a, 2014b). Factors such as mentoring, guiding, emotional, and completion support can improve their doctoral experience (Mantai and Dowling, 2015).

Imposter syndrome is a common experience in any new learning setting. It also occurs in first-generation doctoral students and candidates with industrial backgrounds who know what they are doing and suddenly face the unknown. It includes feelings of self-doubt about intellect, skills, or accomplishments amongst high achievers. Candidates also say that the pressure of always being right and showing up as the best version of yourself is intense. Productivity-progress-orientated programmes exacerbate this, especially when candidates have little room to explore, make mistakes, or learn from them. A number of online fora comments highlight that there is no time to fail. In reality, you cannot fail.

Candidates returning to an academic environment after a long time can expect to experience moments of self-doubt. The question is what to do with it. Do you push it aside and act as if you know what you are doing? Should you be concerned that someone appears to be performing at a higher level or progressing more quickly than you are? A nursing faculty head and supervisor who contributed to the interviews advises that PhD candidates should be mindful of informal WhatsApp/Telegram/Signal groups. They run the risk of turning into venting sessions. Moderated groups, on the other hand, can add value and build a sense of belonging and practical support (Weidman and Stein, 2003; Wisker et al., 2007).

Fear of missing out (FOMO) is another challenge for part-time candidates because they don't have the time to weigh up the pros and cons of activities relating to the PhD, such as networking and connecting with peers.

Interviewees also expressed frustration with the amount of time dealing with bureaucracy, politics, and paperwork, highlighting that the speed of decision-making in academia operates at a different pace than in other areas of life. Some also talked about lab and faculty politics, with one part-time PhD in Social Sciences adding, "I wish had known what I was letting myself in for".

The literature highlights a gap in addressing the needs of "invisible" part-time researchers and that there is not enough time or capacity to explore, discover, and grow (Neumann and Rodwell, 2009). They have little time to connect with the institution; when they do so, it's on a functional basis: "I only go when I have to meet someone or have a review" (Mantai, 2019). There is little time to connect to a network and no time to socialise within an academic environment.

> "Even though I was listed as a faculty member. It did not feel that way. My supervisor invited me to a drinks reception for a retiring colleague. I found it hard to shake off the student-lecturer relationship as it has been many years since I was in education. The reception allowed me to meet with peers, then, I realised we were all in the same boat. Similar insecurities and trying to do our best."
>
> PhD, Communication

Doctoral trends include:

- Increasing time pressure
- Taking a cost-benefit approach to work (Müller, 2014)
- An individualistic culture favouring productivity

The literature points out that there is an emphasis on productivity and progression in current doctoral systems. Moreover, there are calls to refocus institutional support and resources so that they focus on the doctoral candidate and their development rather than the thesis or publication. This proposed approach benefits part-time mature candidates who say, "I'm doing the doctorate for ME" (part-time PhD, History).

▶ WHEEL OF LIFE®

The Wheel of Life® is a visual tool that looks at eight dimensions associated with daily living (see Figure 12.1). It says that when much attention is placed on one area of life, for example, our career, one or more other areas of life are imbalanced.

The literature suggests doctoral student wellbeing is linked to development, facilities, home & health, research, social, supervisor, and university. These factors partially meet the needs of part-time,

EXERCISE: BALANCE

This exercise helps to quickly identify areas of your life that might require special attention during the doctoral programme. Document the first answer that springs to mind.

STEP 1: WHERE AM I NOW?

1. Using the list provided, on a scale of 0 to 10 (where 0 is the lowest and 10 is the highest score), Ask: What mark would I give in this area of my life?
2. Which sections have the highest and lowest scores?
3. Mark the scores with an x in each spoke and join the dots (0 is at the centre of the diagram).
4. Notice the shape:
5. What are the priorities you need to work on?

HEALTH & WELLBEING _____
MONEY _____
CAREER _____
FRIENDS & FAMILY _____
RECREATION & FUN _____
PERSONAL & SPIRITUAL GROWTH _____
PHYSICAL ENVIRONMENT _____
SIGNIFICANT OTHER(S) _____

Figure 12.1 Wheel of Life® Framework Summary. Wheel of Life® is a registered trademark of Success Motivation® International, Inc. © 2023 Sinéad Hewson created with Canva.com

mature, and candidates from under-represented groups. Feedback from candidates is that their institution provides resources and support services orientated towards those working within the institution and in real terms, it is your responsibility to work out the support you need to complete (Juniper et al., 2012). The Wheel of Life® has a broader reach and can help you work out priorities, it is customisable, accessible, easy to use, and relatable.

A PERSONAL PERSPECTIVE

"I was introduced to the Wheel of Life® tool at a time when my professional life was in pretty good shape and my personal circumstances had changed. I had a fantastic career, led an amazing team and was part of a loving and supportive family. I reflected on the reasons why I get up in the morning and felt that things were amazing. I looked at the wheel and gave each segment a score out of ten. In that moment realised that I was getting by rather than thriving. Something had to change, and that something was me."

Author

Health and wellbeing

Taking care of yourself throughout your doctoral programme is about making a list of to-dos to live a healthy life. It means developing a level of self-awareness that allows you to meet the demands of the programme, personal obligations, and professional responsibilities.

Although you are motivated to complete the doctorate, with that comes the recognition that there are temporary changes you need to make to get the work done. Self-care and health come first. This means knowing when to work intensely and when to take time out, knowing when to say no and being aware of triggers that impact performance (Franz, 2012; Dweck, 2017). Establishing a strong support system is critical, as is a proper night's sleep. Most important of all, ask for help (practical help as well as mental health support) when you need it (Dweck, 2017).

Eat a well-balanced diet rich in nutrients, including protein, carbohydrates, vitamins, and minerals. Avoid highly processed convenience food. Hydrate. Drink plenty of water. Avoid stimulants, alcohol, and caffeine.

Incorporate fitness and exercise into your daily routine. Walk or cycle to work. Organise virtual walks and take a walk outdoors daily or at lunch. Take the stairs. Stretch throughout the day. Take a break from your desk every 45–50 minutes and move. Blink. Exercise for fun rather than duty – salsa dancing, perhaps?

Money

Financial health and wellbeing, namely how you spend, save, borrow, and plan before, during, and after your programme, requires careful consideration. The interviews highlighted that there is a negative, short- to medium-term impact on family finances and that any economic benefits are not felt until three, maybe four years after completion. The literature indicated that part-time doctoral candidates' financial support is inconsistent or non-existent, therefore proactively planning helps reduce stress and feelings of financial burden. The interviews also highlighted that potential sources of financial support were clear to them until after they had completed their programme.

Action

1. Develop a monthly budget listing items and typical costs needed to complete the programme and cover day-to-day expenses, equipment, clothing, and treats.
2. Allocate time to research financial supports, bursaries, and grants to help recoup costs.
3. Examine the pros and cons of a loan and funding alternatives to cover the last year of the programme so you can choose whether to work full time for a couple of months to get the doctorate over the finish line.
4. What are your future financial ambitions? How might the doctorate, and your newly acquired skills enable this?

Career

The interviews and literature review highlighted that doctorates believe they become better at their work thanks to the skills and capabilities acquired throughout the process. Also, they do not necessarily wish to remain in academia. As a part-time candidate, take time to explore your career and financial wellbeing during and after the doctoral programme.

Consider the following:

1. In what way might the doctorate advance my career? Do I have an ambition to use it for financial/professional gain?
2. In what way has the programme helped me identify my strengths?
3. What skills have I developed/gained due to the programme?
4. In what way has the doctoral experience helped me diversify and grow my professional network?
5. In what way have I grown professionally?
6. Have my values shifted? What are they?
7. Does my current career path align with my values?
8. Has my purpose changed direction?
9. Does my current career path help me fulfil my purpose?
10. Does my career give me the work-life balance I need to thrive?
11. How might the doctorate help with my current or future work environment?
12. Does the revenue I earn from my career support my lifestyle? What needs to change to do so?

Friends and family

Strong support networks and family are important in many cultures. When you start a PhD, your availability changes. New people enter your world, and those who know you need time to adjust to the new you. Assess the level of commitment required to complete and work out how this will fit around your life. Discuss this openly with loved ones, and know when to connect and disconnect and be prepared to say NO. If support is lacking, discuss this with your supervisor and discuss ways to address this.

Personal and spiritual growth

The doctorate is a journey of transformation and growth. The discomfort the change causes is a natural part of the process and contributes towards your development on a personal, professional and spiritual level.

Reflect on how the doctoral experience has enabled you to grow and live purposefully. In what way specifically has the doctoral experience impacted the guiding principles, beliefs, or values that give you purpose in your life? Consider including elements of this exercise within your thesis and as part of your annual review.

> "Understand the guidance from your supervisors. Listen to their perspective. They understand what the output looks like. Conform and comply."
>
> Part-time PhD through prior publication

If you choose to discontinue or defer your studies, recognise the strength and reasoning behind your decision and acknowledge what the doctoral experience has given you. It is an achievement to gain acceptance to a programme, and recognising that this path is not for you or that a more suitable path has emerged is a sign of maturity and positive growth.

> "Despite [family] support, I felt that it would be too much of a burden. It would mean sacrificing work time and volunteering time. I deferred my studies."
>
> PhD candidate, Law who deferred

Physical environment

Workspace ergonomics considers ways to proactively optimise your work and living space for better comfort, productivity and wellbeing. Taking time throughout your studies to understand how you physically work (posture, height, lighting) means you can recalibrate your desk, chair, computer, and keyboard set-up and carefully place necessary equipment and resources for optimum health, productivity and focus on getting the work done.

First of all, look at your workspace. Is it well set up? Is it comfortable, inviting, and well-lit? Is it easy to access when you need to? Are there enough light fixtures, storage, and power outlets? Do you have adequate access to technology (computer, printer, internet etc.)? It is (reasonably) distraction- and clutter-free, so you can start working with minimal clearing up. Are the floor, shelves, tables, and walls free from papers, filing, and personal items? If your workspace is combined with your living space, can you work distraction-free or around caring and family time?

What about you? Are you aware of your posture, how you type, use your mouse? Do you slouch at your desk? Do your feet touch the ground while sitting at your desk/table?

Needs change, and it is important to review how you work and assess whether your work and living spaces are fit for purpose.

Consider the following:

1. List your basic needs. Reflect on how you work, gather information, and write. Consider how you might set up your space differently to make things easier until the final edits of the doctorate are complete.
2. Do you need a dedicated space? What for, when, and how often?
3. Do you need access to a specialised/unique or quiet area? What for, when, and how often?
4. Do you have access to power sockets, extension leads, and appropriate lighting?
5. Do you have a dedicated desk/workspace/file storage where you can keep work safely online and offline?
6. Is the space organised and (reasonably) tidy?
7. Assess the supplies and resources you need. Do you have access to enough pens, paper, post-its, toner, wall planner, whiteboard, and/or flip chart?

8. Is your computer, headset, keyboard, and mouse fit for purpose?
9. Is your chair, lighting, and desk adjustable/expandable?
10. Are you sitting comfortably? Do you slouch? Do you stretch your neck to see the screen? What about your neck, back, shoulders, wrist, and fingers? Do you stand when at your desk? Do you take regular breaks and stretch?

Multiple resources are available online to set up a home office with limited or no budget. Take a common-sense approach and proactively adjust your workspace throughout the programme. Sedentary lifestyles and poor posture have an impact on long-term health and wellbeing. Own your health and proactively manage it.

Significant others

The Significant Other in the Wheel of Life® refers to the person you are in a serious relationship with, such as a partner, spouse, or loved one and is addressed in the Friends and Family section. It can also refer to any individual who is important for a person's state of wellbeing. Given that the focus of the book is doctoral completion. The supervisor's role and peer-to-peer support are included in this section.

The role of the supervisor

Supervision engagement has a direct impact on completion and quality of the body of work delivered at the end of the doctoral process. Part-time candidates require special attention because the combination of perpetual outsider, first-generation candidacy, and the burden of representation requires understanding, practical support, and a gentle push to finish from supervisors. Mature candidates are naturally proactive, and supervisor behaviours influence their sense of wellbeing and belonging in an unfamiliar academic environment. Interviewees said that supervisors should act as a guide and sparring partner. They should enable the process, signpost, give timely feedback, elicit expectations, and encourage them to keep going.

A MESSAGE TO SUPERVISORS

"Be proactive ... we don't ask to be spoon-fed."

Part-time PhD, Entrepreneurship

Peer-to-peer support

Some institutions organise peer group support sessions, academic writing clinics, and meditation workshops hosted by post-doctoral researchers and experts. There is a drive to develop supportive networks and dialogue-driven teams in research communities. Some initiatives are skills-based, others focus on wellbeing and create opportunities to connect with like-minded people. For example, in my institution, they organise a writing clinic, which is a 30-minute face-to-face meeting with a stranger with a doctorate and from a different faculty. They are tasked with reading, reviewing, and giving feedback on a sample A4 page of text provided in advance by the candidate. It creates an opportunity to talk through the writing process and give feedback on style, form, and completion tips. My mentor was a physicist from India who pointed out that academic discourse is one like-minded academic talking to another on an equal footing. There is no need to impress. The key to academic writing is to concisely communicate in a way that resonates with you and the people you want to connect with.

Informal peer support is powerful too, for example, asking whether there are post-doctorates in the faculty or on campus who are known for using referencing tools and documentation superbly. It only takes a phone call, email, or an introduction to organise a virtual or in-person coffee to pick their brains and ask questions on how they use the tools.

Choose peer groups carefully and be mindful that you don't get caught up in someone else's problem. One supervisor commented in the interviews that "some students may cause undue stress and anxiety as they talk about the challenges of their own journey, which may not apply to you". The type of supportive environments you access has a direct impact on performance, progression, and wellbeing.

INSIGHT

"Sometimes, I couldn't find an article or a reference. Oh man, and I'd say to someone on Focusmate, I'm struggling to find this. They would offer to check it for me and send me the source, you know, so those, and I think Focusmate really did help."

Focusmate partner conversation

▶ WHAT WOULD YOU DO?

The following section contains a number of scenarios to help you reflect and adopt positive, and achievable self-care habits during the doctoral programme. What would you do?

Scenario I. Sleep

I'm lying in bed, staring at the ceiling, while data, hypotheses, and what-ifs dance across my mind. Even though my eyes are closed, I'm wide awake, I hear every rustling blade of grass outside. My partner is in a deep sleep, breathing in sync with the ticking clock on the mantlepiece downstairs. I see layers of citations building one on top of the other while potential arguments, questions, and challenges pop into my thoughts like weeds in a poorly managed yard. All I want to do is do good work and contribute to scholarly discussion. Why is it so hard to break through? It feels like I'm pushing through concrete. Conflicting images and voices jolt me awake. It's 2 am. What should I do?

I can:

1. Sit up, take notes, and capture all my thoughts so that I forget nothing when my conscious mind wakes up at sunrise.
2. Allow the dissenting voices in my head to take over and unpick my research.
3. Shake my partner awake and tell them all about what's going on in my head, the questions, the what-ifs, everything!

4. Take a deep breath and notice how my thoughts bubble, ferment, and play, and when I arise refreshed and rested, I'll put pen to paper and allow the most important points to appear on the page.
5. Allow these thoughts to infiltrate my waking hours. I am pre-occupied and forget the people around me. I hear what they say, but I am not listening to them.

What would you do? There was a time when I fought against these thoughts, now, I see them as a gift, a donation of time to process my thoughts and sleep.

Scenario II. Habits

"Every morning, I free-write, and the jumble that was once in my mind makes perfect sense. Sometimes, it is a long paragraph, and more often, it is a phrase, a sentence bursting with wisdom and a gentle sense of knowing. It is the perfect start (and end) to my day."

Reflect on this statement. What habits can you develop?

Examples of steps I can take to stay organised and focused

1. Use a calendar (use resources within to make things easier).
2. Set up playlists to support your work.
3. Identify tools and resources that make life easier (e.g. Focus-mate, Wunderlust, Evernote etc. (See exercise on finding the right technology).
4. How will the doctorate fit into your life? (Discuss with family, friends and employer.)
5. When is the best time to work on the doctorate (block it in your diary)?

"It's useful to see what others do. There are some who write regularly. It all starts the night before. When you need to write, it helps to go to bed at a reasonable time, avoid excess alcohol, caffeine or other stimulants and get a good night's sleep."

Novelist, former PhD proofreader

What habits and routines work best for you to complete the PhD. What are they specifically? Who can you model or learn from? Integrate them into your way of working.

Scenario III. Support

"When other people offered me their support. I took that support."

Focusmate partner conversation

Reflect on the supports and resources you need, now and into the future. What specifically do you need and how will you access and pay for them?

Scenario IV. Continue, defer, or stop

"I almost stopped everything. I moved country with two young kids. My husband was travelling, I was alone a lot and did not speak the local language. He encouraged me to finish, recognising that this was an important step for me. 'If you don't finish,' he said, 'there will come a day in the future when you will blame us. You have to do this.'"

PhD, Psychology

Reflect on motivating reasons to continue, defer or stop. Who can support you so that you make your decision for the right reasons?

Scenario V. What will it take?

When something matters, it's frightening to put your chips on the table. Life can be a constant distraction. The price is emotional vulnerability. Am I willing to be hurt so that I can be a player? Allow yourself to be vulnerable.

Novelist, former PhD proofreader

You don't necessarily need much time – you just need enough time. We all have enough time, the same 24 hours a day. The key is finding *the right mental state to write*, review data, focus and organise ourselves. I use a marble to represent every page I have written.

Part-time PhD, Communication

Reflect on these two statements. Ask, what will it take to enable the process, enjoy the experience, and complete it?

Scenario VI. Friends and family

"It is also important to find time to do the things you love the most. Build a work routine which also allows you to meet friends for lunch, keep fit and healthy and meet your deadlines and exceed your goals (expectations)."

Novelist, former PhD proofreader

Your family and social life as a part-time PhD student is not that much different from how it would be if you were working a part-time or full-time job and coaching an elite amateur sports team. What steps can you take to fit your family and friends around your academic responsibilities? What will it look like?

Scenario VII. What you say versus what you do

Read this scenario on routines. Do you relate to some or part of them?

What writers say is an ideal routine

Most writers say they write in the morning, maybe arising at 07:30, drinking a fresh green smoothie and tea. Then they go to their writing space, work for 4 hours and eat breakfast at their desk.

How I say I work

I aim to be at my desk by 8 am and write first followed by journalling planning my day and then I focus on a piece of work. I write in short bursts, capture my work in a folder and move things around. I (1) re-read my work from the day before, (2) edit, (3) write a chapter a day, (4) sit and eat, (5) I'm done by noon.

What really happens

I'll be lucky if I start by lunchtime. Then I feel guilty. I use writing group or Focusmate to work in 50-minute bursts. It's free, might share a goal or an inspirational quote. Then everyone writes. I focus on what I am writing, and I do this four times a day.

I used Scrivener to craft my first draft. It's the only place where I wrote. I go to the pages every morning, and I journal. I outline my worries and fears and say in bold letters YES, I CAN. It works for me. It gets me started.

I use my diary to block out writing slots in chunks of time. I always say I'll complete it by noon and then work for the afternoon. The reality is I am delayed and distracted, and I end up working for the afternoon and into the evening and the writing gets bumped to the next day.

I use timers to work in small blocks of 15 minutes or even 1 minute. I also have a sand timer on my desk.

▶ FIND WAYS OF WORKING THAT SUIT YOU

Ask:

1. What kind of person am I like? How do I work? How do I eat?
2. Track how you work to get a better understanding of this.

Exercise: Track my word count/activity

Setting a word count on a daily/weekly basis helps you keep on track with where you are in the process (Table 12.1). Keep this task simple. Use it to summarise and acknowledge your daily/weekly achievements.

TABLE 12.1 Track my word count/activity

DATE	TIME I STARTED	WORD COUNT	NOTES (What I did)

Scenario VIII. Keep going

Sometimes, you are in a state where you can barely touch your research or look at your manuscript.

Do you:

1. Make yourself open it. Start in the middle of an existing file and then build up slowly into the work?
2. Get two jars – one empty, the other full of marbles. Put one into a bowl – every 100 words.
3. Take a break.

Self-care is what people do for themselves to establish and maintain health and prevent and deal with illness. In this scenario, what are the best choices for you? Write down what they are and why.

▶ SUMMARY

The Wheel of Life® framework was used to explore *wellbeing*, the fourth doctoral completion trigger, and several "what would you do?" scenarios presented to help candidates develop a state of awareness of what wellbeing means and the role it plays in completing a doctorate.

The themes covered this this chapter are:

Career
Friends and Family

Habits
Health and Wellbeing
Keeping going
Money
Personal and Spiritual Growth
Physical Environment
Significant Others
The role of the supervisor
Wellbeing
Wheel of Life®

▶ USEFUL RESOURCES AND REFERENCES

References

Archer, L. (2008). Younger academics' constructions of "authenticity", "success" and professional identity. *Studies in Higher Education, 33* (4), 385–403. doi:10.1080/03075070802211729

Dweck, C. S. (2017). *Mindset - Updated edition: Changing the way you think to fulfil your potential.* London: Little, Brown Book Group: Kindle Edition: ISBN: 978-1-47213-996-2.

Franz, T. M. (2012). *Group dynamics and team interventions. Understanding and improving team performance.* (1st ed., pp. 160–162). Oxford: Wiley-Blackwell: ISBN: 1405186771.

Gardner, S. K., & Holley, K. A. (2011). "Those invisible barriers are real": The progression of first-generation students through doctoral education. *Equity & Excellence in Education, 44* (1), 77–92. doi:10. 1080/10665684.2011.529791

Juniper, B., Walsh, E., Richardson, A., & Morley, B. (2012). A new approach to evaluating the wellbeing of PhD research students. *Assessment & Evaluation in Higher Education, 37* (5), 563–576. doi:10.1080/02602938.2011.555816

Mantai, L. (2019). 'A source of sanity': The role of social support for doctoral candidates' belonging and becoming. *International Journal of Doctoral Studies, 14,* 367–382. doi:10.28945/4275

Mantai, L., & Dowling, R. (2015). Supporting the PhD journey: Insights from acknowledgements. *International Journal for Researcher Development, 6* (2), 106–121. doi:10.1108/IJRD-03-2015-0007

Müller, R. (2014). Racing for what? Anticipation and acceleration in the work and career practices of academic life science postdocs. *Forum Qualitative Sozialforschung Forum: Qualitative Social Research, 15* (3). doi:10.17169/fqs-15.3.2245

Neumann, R., & Rodwell, J. (2009). The "invisible" part-time research students: A case study of satisfaction and completion. *Studies in Higher Education, 34* (1), 55–68. doi:10.1080/03075070802601960

Neumann, R., & Tan, K. K. (2011). From PhD to initial employment: The doctorate in a knowledge economy. *Studies in Higher Education, 36* (5), 601–614. doi:10.1080/03075079.2011.594596

Peltonen, J. A., Vekkaila, J., Rautio, P., Haverinen, K., & Pyhältö, K. (2017). Doctoral students' social support profiles and their relationship to burnout, drop-out intentions, and time to candidacy. *International Journal of Doctoral Studies, 12*, 157–173. doi:10.28945/3792

Shavers, M., & Moore, J. L., III. (2014a). Black female voices: Self- presentation strategies in doctoral programs at predominately White institutions. *Journal of College Student Development, 55*, 391–407. doi:10. 1353/csd.2014.0040

Shavers, M., & Moore, J. L., III. (2014b). The double edge sword: Coping and resiliency strategies of African American women enrolled in doctoral programs at predominately White institutions. *Frontiers: A Journal of Women Studies, 35*, 15–38. doi:10.1353/fro.2014.0039

Shavers, M. C., & Moore, J. L. (2019). The perpetual outsider: Voices of black women pursuing doctoral degrees at predominantly white institutions. *Journal of Multicultural Counseling and Development, 47* (4), 210–226. doi:10.1002/jmcd.12154

Trevitt, C., & Perera, C. (2009). Self and continuing professional learning (development): Issues of curriculum and identity in developing academic practice. *Teaching in Higher Education, 14* (4), 347–359. doi:10.1080/13562510903050095

Weidman, J. C., & Stein, E. L. (2003). Socialization of doctoral students to academic norms. *Research in Higher Education, 44* (6), 641–656. doi:10.1023/A:1026123508335

Wisker, G., Robinson, G., & Shacham, M. (2007). Postgraduate research success: Communities of practice involving cohorts, guardian supervisors and online communities. *Innovations in Education and Teaching International, 44* (3), 301–320. doi:10.1080/14703290701486720

Resources

WHO website. http://apps.who.int/iris/handle/10665/205887

PhD.me website. https://www.phds.me/resources/doctoral-student-health-and-wellness/

Workspace and Ergonomic resources and trends. https://ergonomictrends.com/ergonomic-research/

13 Conclusion

▶ I HAVE MY DOCTORATE. NOW WHAT?

As a doctoral candidate, completing a significant project over a prolonged period of time is one of the requirements to secure the degree. Once you have reached your goal, catch your breath and consider what's next. Brainstorming a bucket list Table 13.1 is a good start. Stay true to yourself and do what's right for you, even if it means stepping out of your comfort zone. Remain curious, use your imagination and be specific. For instance, if you consider sky-diving or visiting a historic location, what would that look like? Will you be alone or with someone? Pay attention to what excites or scares you and find ways to make your goals a reality.

This part of the journey is all about you.

INSIDER TIPS

Living with the doctorate and thesis. Take time to let go and rethink your dreams. You have been living with the doctorate for many years. Completion is like a child moving out of the house. This creates a sense of emptiness and loss. Acknowledge it.

DOI: 10.4324/9781003413691-17

TABLE 13.1 Exercise: Bucket list

Step 1:

You've completed your doctorate and secured one of the highest awards possible. Well done! What happens next?

1. Brainstorm 100 things you want to experience in the next decade. Ask: Wouldn't it be great if I …

Step 2:

Reflect and ask:

2. How do I make it happen, and when?
3. What resources do I need?
4. Can I combine ideas into a trip, a location, or a theme?
5. Can you tick off an item in the next month, quarter, six months, or year?
6. Make a list and create a mind map or vision board. Play with the ideas. Notice what comes up.

Step 3:

Identify three next steps to bring your ideas to fruition.

1.

2.

3.

Bucket List © 2023 Sinéad Hewson.

▶ ONE FINAL THOUGHT

I wrote the guide because the needs of unconventional doctoral candidates (i.e. individuals from underrepresented groups and those without an academic background, self-funded, not working in education or part-time) are not fully addressed within their institutions. The experiences of those who shared their insights in the book will, I hope, inspire potential candidates to believe they can apply for and complete a doctorate utilising practical life experience, deliver a body of work, and create new knowledge that is both meaningful and relevant. The book is structured to help them focus, organise, and keep going.

I interviewed potential candidates, those going through the process, those who stopped, and those who completed their programme. They said they need access to useful information, experts who understand their situation, independent mentorship, peer support, and common-sense tools.

Several trends emerged while researching this book: first of all, completion rates. The problem is that 50% of doctoral candidates in the US and 25% in the Netherlands don't complete their programmes. The risk is even higher if you come from an underrepresented group or, like me, are self-funded and work outside academia. There are calls for wider representation in, for example, the composition of expert groups assessing funding programmes in Europe, the make-up of executive boards, and the nature of funded start-ups and their founders. Diversifying the doctoral talent pool may help this.

Second of all, the issue of imbalance, over-, and under-representation. For example, in 2022, six out of every ten doctorates in the US were awarded to white candidates, and gender imbalance (although improving) remains in the latest global data on doctoral programme registrations. It is time for sustainable change.

Third, there is a gap in the relevance of academic research versus real-world application. Some scholars propose that 85% of research funding is wasted and that there is a need for better, more relevant research that is performed for the right reasons. The untapped potential of candidates leveraging lived experience to develop impactful new knowledge is significant. For instance, they could examine the impact of workarounds in highly specialised work environments and convert them into innovations in wound care, fire safety management, waste management, and grass-root climate change actions.

It also picks up on market growth and increased participation trends. The global doctoral market has grown by 18% since 2010, and at the same time, opportunities for candidates to participate and engage in the doctoral process have increased. so that candidates who were at risk of dropping out in the past could, with the right know-how, resources, and support, complete their programmes.

I hope the book resonates with and builds self-belief in doctoral candidates, encouraging them to participate, innovate, and contribute to new knowledge. I hope that they recognise their capability, trust themselves, and aim high. My wish is that employers, professional, and trade bodies spot talented individuals within their networks, and then fund and enable them to experience the doctoral process first-hand so they can give back to their sector. This book can become a practical resource for supervisors, promoters, and graduate research departments supporting independent candidates who need signposting, not hand-holding.

Your feedback is welcome. I'd love to hear from you.

1. What was the doctoral experience like?
2. Do you have advice or tips you want to share?
3. Did you complete or stop?

I can be reached at sineadhewson@tpebo.com or info@uncon ventionaldoctorates.com and on LinkedIn www.linkedin.com/in/ hewson.

Stay humble. Dream BIG.

With best wishes

Sinéad Hewson
Voorschoten, The Netherlands

INSIGHT

"The doctorate changed my thinking and I became even better at what I do."

Part-time PhD, Social Psychology

▶ SUMMARY

The guide focused on doctoral completion triggers of *motivation, organisation, progress,* and *wellbeing,* which were identified when researching the book and hoped to mitigate the risk of dropping out. A PhD is an immersive, consuming experience. The closing chapter acknowledges that there is a time to let go, to grieve, and then re-imagine a new future and what to do next. The journey starts with a post-doctoral bucket list.

▶ USEFUL RESOURCES AND REFERENCES

Resources

Bucket list ideas. https://www.bucketlist.net/life-goals/
The Times Higher Education. https://www.timeshighereducation.com/campus/thinking-about-quitting-your-phd-maybe-thats-right-decision

▶ PS

Close to the manuscript submission deadline for this book, I hit a wall and re-read the notes, interviews, and conversations of people who wanted to help me complete it. Their stories reminded me to connect with the reason why I want this book to exist. The why was unchanged, to help under-represented and part-time candidates complete, and the "How do I make this happen?" shifted. At the start of the process, the book focused on addressing the unmet needs of doctoral candidates outside of education, highlighted the gaps, and was academically orientated. In the closing stages, I deleted most of the material and focused on providing genuinely useful content that aids completion. The tone of voice changed to one that positions a doctoral programme as an empowering, transformational experience regardless of the outcome. I had pangs of guilt when I missed the original deadline, but I had to stop, focus on the why, and re-write the book.

Your why can be hard to put into words. The answer, I believe, lies closer to the soul than the ego, it is an inner sense of knowing and unique to you.

When you find your why, anything is possible ❤

Index

Pages in *italics* refer to figures and pages in **bold** refer to tables.

Printed in the United States
by Baker & Taylor Publisher Services